W9-BTA-447

GREAT BEER FROM KITS

Joe Fisher and Dennis Fisher

A Storey Publishing Book

STOREY

Storey Communications, Inc.
Schoolhouse Road
Pownal, Vermont 05261

*The mission of Storey Communications is to serve our customers
by publishing practical information that encourages personal independence
in harmony with the environment.*

Edited by Lee Harrison and Pamela Lappies
Cover design by Greg Imhoff
Text design by Cynthia McFarland
Text production by Susan Bernier and Cynthia McFarland
Line drawings by Alison Kolesar
Indexed by Northwind Editorial Services

Copyright © 1996 by Dennis and Joseph A. Fisher

The information in this book is true and complete to the best of our knowledge. All recommendations are made without guarantee on the part of the author or Storey Communications, Inc. The author and publisher disclaim any liability in connection with the use of this information. For additional information please contact Storey Communications, Inc., Schoolhouse Road, Pownal, Vermont 05261.

Printed in the United States by Book Press

10 9 8 7 6 5 4 3 2 1

Library of Congress Cataloging-in-Publication Data

Fisher, Joe, 1966–
    Great beer from kits / Joe Fisher and Dennis Fisher.
              p.   cm.
    "A Storey Publishing book."
    Includes bibliographical references and index.
    ISBN 0-88266-911-7 (alk. paper)
    1. Brewing—Amateurs' manuals.   I. Fisher, Dennis, 1963–   .
II. Title.
    TP570.F54   1996
    641.8'73—dc20   95-33254
                                                              CIP

DEDICATION

To the Märtens:
Rolf, Ingie, Olaf, Axel, Ute, and Omi.

ACKNOWLEDGMENTS

This book was written in collaboration with Ben Gleason and Don Wagoner of Stout Billy's, our local homebrew store in Portsmouth, NH. Ben and Don provided lots of useful advice and encouragement, designed and tested most of the recipes, and patiently went over the drafts. We would also like to thank Scott and Bill Nelson, owners of Stout Billy's, for their enthusiastic support.

The American Homebrewers' Association and Dena Nisheka of *Zymurgy* helped us, and we are indebted to the authors listed in the bibliography, especially Jill Singleton. We would like to express our thanks to our editors at Storey Communications, including Amanda Haar, for suggesting this project, Gwen Steege, and Pamela Lappies. Special thanks to Kate Giordano for finding us all of those books, and to Nancy Noble for *1000 Remarkable Facts about Booze*.

To our parents, Rose and Jerry Fisher, for their support with this and many other projects, and to Sue Roberts, much thanks.

Contents

NOTE: Words in the text that appear as *boldface italic* are defined in the Glossary beginning on page 153.

Welcome to the Wonderful World of Kit Brewing

KIT BREWING is one of the most popular methods of making beer at home because it is the simplest. Most homebrewers start out this way, and though some move on to other forms of brewing, many never leave the fold because they like the convenience, ease, and confidence of brewing from a kit.

In this book we use the term "kit" to refer to a can of liquid *malt extract*. (Equipment is something else, and we will cover the equipment you need to make great beer from kits later on.) Some homebrew stores put a number of brewing ingredients — malt grains, malt extract, and hops — into a package and call that a kit, but in this book a kit is simply a can of malt extract formulated to produce the color, the *body*, and the characteristics of a particular type of beer. Such kits simplify homebrewing, and that is the reason we focus solely on them.

To contribute bitterness, hops in some form have been added to most kits. What kind of hops, and how many, depends on the manufacturer and the style. Some add only hop extract, which bitters beer nicely but adds no *aroma* or flavor. A few makers use whole hops, pelletized hops, and hop oils to lend better hop character to the beer. However, the heat and vacuum involved in the canning process tend to drive off the delicate volatile oils responsible for hop aroma and flavor. If you want your beer to have these qualities, you have to add your own hops.

Some kits can make fine beer just as they come off the shelves, and this is especially true of styles that aren't supposed to have much hop character. Some kits need help to achieve perfection. Many can serve as the foundation of one or more superior brews, each as remarkable in its own way as the most expensive microbrewed or imported product. When you factor in the advantages of low cost and the personal touch homebrewing brings, you will soon find yourself preferring your own efforts over all others.

The fact that you started from a kit instead of from scratch makes no difference. It is still your beer, hand-crafted, and, in its own way, unique. Even using the same kit, no two brewers work exactly the same way in exactly the same conditions. Small differences in technique and in the home brewery environment add a "house flavor" to any beer that can't be duplicated elsewhere.

Not only is kit brewing the perfect choice for beginners — and for people who want to brew but don't think they have the time — but it also opens up to the homebrewer a diversity of styles that could otherwise only be appreciated by buying expensive imported beers or by brewing complex recipes. With kits, homebrewed versions of most imports can be produced at roughly half the cost of the original, and they will be fresher for having been made at home.

Kit brewing is also great for making beer under "survival conditions": if your kitchen is very small and you don't have a lot of equipment, if you're living on a boat (don't laugh, people have done this) or an RV, or if you are miles from the nearest large homebrew store and have to make do with a dealer who handles brewsupplies on the side. The kit gives you the flexibility to brew almost anywhere.

Many people are afraid to try homebrewing because they think it is too complicated. Some try it once, fail, and never go back. But with kits you can get your feet wet in homebrewing with little risk of failure. You only need to follow a few simple procedures and rules of cleanliness to ensure success in kit brewing time and again.

A LITTLE BACKGROUND

It is helpful for the beginning homebrewer to know something about what beer is and how it is made. Beer is a subtle phenomenon, a deep alchemy of chemical reactions all working in harmony to produce exactly the right characteristics of flavor, aroma, body, and essence. Ideally, the brewer controls every aspect of brewing from the time the grain is sown until the beer glass is upended, but today most commercial brewing and advanced homebrewing starts after the maltster has finished the job of turning *barley* into *malt*. This is accomplished by sprouting the grains, kilning them, and finally roasting them to the desired color. Then the brewer takes over.

Brewing begins by extracting *sweet wort* or *sweet liquor* from malt grains — a process referred to as *mashing*. In this process the grains are steeped at the correct temperatures and pH for a specified time until the malt starches are converted to sugars that can be fermented into beer. These sugars are rinsed from the mash through a process called *sparging* and *lautering*, in which water at 170°F (77°C) trickles through the grains and is collected as sweet wort.

Hops are then added to the sweet wort — or simply, the *wort* — during a long boil of 1–1½ hours, which sterilizes the wort and liberates the hop *alpha* and *beta acids*. The timing, type, and amount of hops added to the wort are crucial to the style of beer being produced. Boiling hops, for instance, adds bittering characteristics to the beer. Other hops can be added near the end of the boil to enhance flavor or aroma. Creative use of a variety of hops can add great character to beer.

However, in extract brewing — a simpler type of brewing that includes kit brewing — the homebrewer sidesteps the entire mashing process by using liquid malt extract. This is a sweet liquor that has been concentrated in a vacuum at a low temperature to make a thick syrup containing about 10 percent water. Extracts are available with or without hops. Kits, on the other hand, are cans of hopped malt extract that have been formulated to produce a particular kind of beer, further simplifying the homebrewing process.

FROM NO ALTERNATIVE . . .

Homebrewing with extract has been around for a long time. During this country's benighted experiment with prohibition, one of the few ways average folks could keep a supply of potables on hand was to make it themselves. The few lucky souls (and assorted mobsters) with access to wild hops and real beer *yeast* could make a very passable product, but most people had to content themselves with a very hazardous brew derived from ingredients that they could purchase legally in the local market. The recipes varied a little but usually went something like this:

OL' PROHIBITION BRAU

5 gallons water (19L)
1 can Blue Ribbon hopped malt extract
5 pounds white table sugar or brown sugar (2.3 kg)
  hops (if you can get them)
1–2 cakes Fleishman's yeast

Boil the malt extract and sugar in a gallon of water, and then pour the result into a 6-gallon (23L) stoneware crock. Add 4 gallons (15L) of water and crumble the yeast cakes into the wort. Set the uncovered crock behind the old cast-iron wood stove in the kitchen to ferment. Check regularly. Soon the yeast will begin to work and will build up a huge, crusty bloom of froth on top of the wort. After a week or so (depending on the season) the foam will fall and submerge into the crock. Wash and dry some bottles. Using a dipper and funnel, fill the bottles and cap.

Ol' Prohibition needed to be drunk up quickly, before the bottles started to explode. Only about two batches in three would be successful, because no one understood the need for rigorous sanitation in the home brewery. The beer was golden, strong, and cidery, with a suggestion of bread yeast. At its best, Prohibition brew wasn't bad, especially if you had nothing else to drink.

The times are better now. Since 1979 homebrewing has been legal, and a wide variety of supplies and ingredients are available to meet your every brewing need.

. . . To a World of Choice

When you walk into a homebrew store for the first time, you will probably see an overwhelming variety of ingredients, books, and equipment. Somewhere in all of this profusion, you will find shelves of multicolored kits. Some very small brew stores stock kits almost exclusively.

The number of styles of beer kits can be daunting. Most kits come from the British Isles, Belgium, or Germany and represent the styles of those regions. The variety available is one reason people like kits. You can make something unusual or something basic — a full-bodied European *ale* or a light American *lager*. Some kits offer odd and unusual styles such as cherry kriek, raspberry framboise, and diabolo that one might not ordinarily try. Exciting and unusual beers brewed relatively inexpensively at home — isn't that why we became homebrewers?

Beer style is determined by a great many factors: the kind of malts used, the hops, and even the type of yeast. The two major styles of beer are ales and lagers, and both are available in kits.

Ales are "top-fermenting" — that is, after fermenting the beer, the yeast rises to the top of the fermenting vessel. Ale yeasts need warm temperatures — 55° to 75°F (13°–24°C), preferably

65° to 70°F (18–21°C) — in order to act and complete their *fermentation* quickly. British brewers specialize in ales, a type of beer that includes stouts and porters.

Lagers originated in Germany. Lager yeasts are bottom-fermenting. They like cold temperatures and take a long time to act. "Lagering" means aging, and this was done in cold cellars and caves and could take months. A beer like a Märzen, which is brewed in March, would be drunk in October. Though there is as much variety in lagers as in ales, the flavor of lager tends to be subtler and cleaner.

Most U.S. microbreweries today favor ales, which are quick to brew and are easy to keep on tap. Microbrewed beers are often, but not exclusively, dark and rich European-style brews, though there are plenty of lighter beers to be found. So if you are looking to duplicate microbrewed taste, you may want to try these styles.

Whatever style of beer you decide to brew, you will undoubtedly be impressed with how good it tastes. And since you can control factors like aging and *conditioning* in your own beer cellar, your beer will always be served at its best and freshest. That isn't always the case at a microbrewery, where the demand is such (especially in the summer months) that sometimes the beer isn't aged as long as it should be. A fresh beer, one that does not taste stale or old, is of course desirable. But a brew that is too young tastes raw and unfinished; the living yeasts have not had time to complete their life cycle and bring the beer to perfection. Beers need time to condition, and, especially in the stronger brews, the flavors need to blend and mellow with age.

INGREDIENTS

Your first step is to pick a kit, and many people begin brewing with a basic English ale. The beer renaissance really started in England in 1971 with the formation of the Campaign for Real Ale (CAMRA). Later it spread to the United States, as a kind of backlash against bland commercial beers. So raise your glasses to the English, who gave us back great flavor!

English ale is a simple-to-brew and tasty beer, and there is a large number of kits for this style. Most of them are, of course, British, which means that the hops and malts used to produce the kit are all authentic. The English use a different form of barley malt than is usually found in America. Their barley has 2 rows of kernels per head, which yields a larger grain with different characteristics than the 6-row barley used here in America. The English also use just a few varieties of hops, generally East Kent Goldings and Fuggles.

Kits come in a variety of sizes and may contain one or two cans. Small single-can kits range in size from 3.5 to 4 pounds (1.6–1.8 kg); larger single-can kits range from 6.6 to 7 pounds (3–3.1 kg). Double (two-can) kits, and some of the large single-can kits, contain enough malt extract to make a standard 5-gallon (19L) batch of beer without adding anything to them. With the smaller kits it is necessary to add some fermentables to make a 5-gallon batch.

It is fairly standard to add a couple of pounds of malt extract to any kit to boost the body and strength of the beer. Some kits recommend using ordinary cane or table sugar (sucrose), but this is not a good idea because it thins the beer and adds unpleasant cidery flavors.

All about Yeast

Make sure when you buy your kit that the yeast packet has been refrigerated and isn't out of date. You want the yeast to be fresh, or it will not work the way it is supposed to. Living yeast starts to deteriorate after only a few weeks out of the refrigerator, so if you have any doubts about the yeast, buy a fresh packet, and always keep an extra packet on hand in case of emergencies.

If you are brewing a lager, you will have to buy a separate packet of lager yeast. The yeast provided in kits is usually a top-fermenting ale yeast. Kit suppliers probably do this for the sake of convenience. It takes only a short time for ale yeast to ferment. If you use the yeast provided to ferment your lager, the resulting beer may very well taste like a lager (after all, the kit was formulated to do just that), but it will be an ale. If you ferment it at cold temperatures, the yeast will probably just go to sleep, and you will get incomplete fermentation.

The yeast in homebrew and most microbrewed beers is alive, and this is one reason they taste so much fresher than the store-bought variety. Packaged yeast consists of thousands of tiny, dormant, one-celled fungi. When you add, or *pitch,* the yeast to warm water that is saturated with the kinds of things that yeast eat, namely sugars, it wakes up and starts eating and reproducing like mad. As by-products of all this activity, yeast produces the alcohol, carbon dioxide, and some of the flavors of beer. This is the same process that bakers use when making bread, and, in fact, beer and bread are closely related and were invented at about the same time in ancient Mesopotamia. Since then the yeast strains have diverged, and beer yeasts are now highly specialized. So never substitute bread yeast for beer yeast, even in a dire emergency. You always have time to get to the beer store if your beer yeast fails to activate.

EQUIPMENT, BRIEFLY

Once you have chosen a kit, you need the necessary equipment. Beginning brewers most often buy an equipment set for between $45 and $65. Such a set usually includes:

Two plastic buckets — the *primary fermenter* and the *secondary fermenter/bottling bucket*
A glass *hydrometer* for measuring the *specific gravity* of the beer
A bottle brush
A bottle capper and caps
A *fermentation lock*

Plastic tubing
A filler wand
A chemical sanitizing agent.

We will describe the uses of all of these things in the next chapter.

The equipment set is a good value for the beginning homebrewer. It provides almost everything you will need, minimizing confusion as well as your initial investment. Later, you may want to add other equipment such as *carboys* and bottle washers that will make your brewing more efficient and easier, but you don't need them at first.

You will, however, need some items that are not included in your equipment set:

A large pot for boiling the wort
A long metal or plastic spoon (wood is difficult to sanitize completely)
A fine-mesh kitchen strainer
A cooking thermometer (temperature range 70° to 195°F, 21° to 91°C).

Everything else you need to brew beer you can probably find in your kitchen.

Finally, you will need bottles. These can be some you have collected, or you can buy new ones from the brew store (usually a fairly expensive route unless you get them on sale) or from a bottle redemption or distribution center. Used bottles are cheap, just a few dollars a case, but you will have to clean them yourself. Usually two cases per batch of beer will do it, but it's always wise to prepare a few more than you think you will need. You may make more beer than you expect to, or you may break a bottle. However and wherever you find them, get solid-neck bottles, the type that requires an opener, not the twist-off kind. Also, make sure they are made of colored glass, which screens out light and protects the contents. Beer in clear bottles can become light-struck when exposed to sunlight. This happens when the hops, which are strongly affected by the sun, deteriorate and make the beer taste peculiar.

Brown bottles screen out the greatest amount of ultraviolet light, so they are the best kind to use. Green bottles are not as opaque as brown ones, but they are much better than clear glass, which should only be used as a last resort. Beer should never sit in strong light under any circumstances.

The bottles must be thoroughly cleaned, and their labels must be removed. This task is made easier by soaking them for a few days in 5-gallon (19L) buckets in a mild bleach solution. Boiling the bottles also works well.

THE BEER STORE: YOUR RESOURCE

A beer store is not just a place to buy things; it is a resource for information and advice — a place to meet other brewers, enter contests, exchange recipes, and find out how to join local homebrew societies. We hope your beer store people are cheerful, friendly types who will answer any questions you have about making beer. After all, that is what they are there to do. They understand that beginning brewers panic and call the beer store at least once during their first brewing experience. It is normal and expected.

Basic brewing should be simple, and it should be fun. Don't let yourself get overwhelmed. Just relax, pay attention, follow the steps, and make great beer.

1

BASIC BREWING TECHNIQUES

WHEN WE SAY BASIC, that is what we mean. This is the foolproof procedure for brewing great beer from kits using only the most elementary ingredients and equipment. Later on, we'll get a little more complicated and show you some intermediate recipes and some advanced tools and techniques. But for now we will keep things simple. Be sure to read the entire chapter and become familiar with all the steps before you begin to brew.

Many people start brewing with a simple English bitter like Scrum Rugger, a fairly mild bitter with medium body, delicate hop flavor, and low alcohol content. It should be ready to bottle within a week of brewing and ready to drink within two weeks of bottling. The great thing about bitter is that it gives you results right away, without a lot of suspense, so you'll know within a few weeks if it came out all right.

First, we'll give you the recipe for Scrum Rugger. This is a specific recipe for a particular brew. Then we'll give you the list of basic equipment, followed by the beer-brewing steps in detail. These procedures can be applied to any beer in this book.

Once you have gone through the process, you should not be intimidated by other recipes, no matter how complicated they may seem.

SCRUM RUGGER BITTER

INITIAL GRAVITY: 1.035–1.042   FINAL GRAVITY: 1.014–1.016

3.5 pounds Geordie Bitter kit (1.6 kg)
1½ pounds plain light dry malt extract (.7 kg)
½ ounce East Kent Goldings hop plug (14 g)
1–2 packets Nottingham ale yeast
½ cup corn sugar (125 ml) or 1 cup dry malt extract (180 ml) for priming

---

BASIC BREWING EQUIPMENT

To brew beer from kits you will need (see Chapter 4 for more details):

- **Brew pot** — Any 16- to 20-quart (15–19L) pot will do. Stainless steel, enameled steel, or copper pots are all fine. Most brewers do not recommend aluminum, but the dangers have probably been exaggerated. Use whatever you have.

- **Saucepan** — For boiling the hop rinsing water.

- **Long-handled metal or plastic stirring spoon.**

- **Plastic fermenting bucket with lid** — The 6.7-gallon (25L) plastic fermenter that comes with the equipment set. You will not need the smaller plastic bottling bucket at this point.

- **Fermentation lock** — A small, clear-plastic airlock that isolates your beer from the outside world and serves as a valve to allow fermentation gases to escape.

- **Fine-mesh kitchen strainer** — For straining the hops out of the wort.

- **Plastic hydrometer tube** — You will need this to take a sample of wort for your hydrometer reading.

- **Hydrometer** — A graduated glass instrument that measures the specific gravity of your beer wort.

- **Thermometer** — For telling when it is safe to pitch the yeast (add it to the wort). Yeasts are delicate organisms that can only stand a limited temperature range.

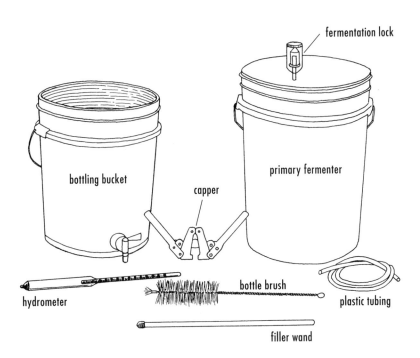

Equipment set

BASIC KIT BREWING:
THE STEPS IN DETAIL

This section gives a detailed description of how to brew beer using a kit. You'll find a quick-reference checklist summarizing these same steps in a box on page 20.

1. Sanitize your plastic fermenting bucket, lid, long-handled spoon, fermentation lock, thermometer, plastic tube, strainer, and hydrometer in a weak solution of household bleach. This is one of the most important steps in homebrewing. Careful attention to cleanliness will guarantee success time after time; sloppy sanitation procedures will eventually lead to disappointment. It is not difficult to start off right. One or 2 tablespoons (15–30 ml) of bleach per gallon (4L) of cool water should do the trick. The easiest way we have found is to mix up the sanitizing solution right in the fermenter, and soak all the other equipment in it. Rinse off your equipment thoroughly with hot water, which will remove the chlorine (and destroy its sanitizing properties). Be careful not to recontaminate your equipment (by laying it down on an unsanitized surface, for instance). It is simplest to leave the equipment in the sanitizing solution until just before you need it, and then rinse it off.

2. Add 1½ gallons (6L) of cold water to your fermenter and chill. Chilling the water helps get the temperature of the beer down to the point where you can pitch the yeast more quickly. Also, it promotes a good **cold break**, which results in a clearer beer. You will need a fairly big refrigerator for this. Just be careful to seal the lid and affix the fermentation lock, because refrigerators are the natural habitat of wild microorganisms that can spoil your beer. Of course, if you're brewing in winter, just set the bucket outside in the snow.

3. Remove the label from the can of malt extract and immerse the can unopened in warm water. Malt extract syrup has the consistency of chilled molasses and is stiff and hard to work with. The warm bath will make the syrup easier to pour and mix with water. Leave the can in the water for about 10 minutes.

4. **Bring 1½ gallons (6L) of water to a boil in the brew pot.** In a separate saucepan, bring ½ gallon (2L) of hop rinsing water to a boil. After the hop rinsing water has boiled, lower the heat to keep it from boiling away to nothing.

5. **Add malt extract to the brew pot and boil for 20 minutes.** After the water comes to a boil, remove the brew pot from the heat. Pour the malt extract into the brew pot and scrape extract away from the sides of the can. Add hot water to the can and stir to dissolve any remaining malt extract and pour it into the brew pot. Add dry malt extract, stirring well to dissolve, and begin to boil the mixture. During boiling, stir occasionally to keep the syrup from burning.

Pouring the extract

NOTE: Boiling is very important. Some kit manufacturers leave out this step or claim it is optional. You must boil the wort, or it could be ruined by wild yeasts or unwanted bacteria.

6. **After boiling the wort for 15 minutes, add hops to the wort and continue boiling for another 5 minutes (total boil time is 20 minutes).** When the wort has boiled for 15 minutes, add the East Kent Goldings hop plug. The hops will contribute flavor and aroma to the beer.

7. **Strain boiled wort into fermenter.** Carefully pour the boiled wort through the strainer into the fermenter, which

Straining the wort

contains 1½ gallons (6L) of chilled water.

8. **Rinse the hops with boiled water.** Pour hot water from the saucepan over the hops and gently press the hops with your spoon. This will squeeze out any wort and hop essences remaining in the hops. If some hops get into the fermenter, don't worry. They will settle out.

9. **Add enough cold water to the fermenter to make up 5 gallons (19L).** On a standard primary fermenter bucket, the 5-gallon mark is indicated by the thick plastic collar. Once you have 5 gallons in the fermenter, stir the liquid with your sanitized metal spoon to mix in the wort.

10. **Take a hydrometer reading.** Using the sanitized plastic tube, wine thief, or turkey baster, take a sample of the wort. Cool it to 60°F (16°C) and take a hydrometer reading (see "How to Use the Hydrometer," on page 18). This is your initial specific gravity. Write it down.

11. **When the wort has cooled to 75°F (24°C), pitch (add) the yeast.** Rinse your sanitized thermometer and shake it down; otherwise it will give you a false reading. Take the wort's temperature — 90°F (32°C) and up is lethal to yeast. A few degrees above 75°F (24°C) is okay, and if the temperature is lower than 75°F (24°C), you are ready to pitch. Immersing the fermenter in a cold water bath can help bring down the wort temperature quickly. When the temperature is right, add the yeast and stir it in with the sanitized spoon.

12. Attach the fermentation lock and place the lid on the fermenter. To attach the fermentation lock, you must sanitize one hand. (Dip your hand in the sanitizing solution and rinse; unsanitized hands can be dangerous to beer. If you don't want bleach on your hands, wear rubber gloves.) Then put the sanitized hand on the inside of the cover and carefully press the stem of the lock through the gasket. Seal the lid, and shake the bucket gently to aerate the wort. This will introduce oxygen the yeast needs for reproduction.

13. Ferment for 7 to 10 days. Move your fermenting bucket to a quiet spot — out of direct light — with temperatures between 65° and 70°F (18°–21°C) for ale, or between 40° and 50°F (4°–10°C) for lager. A plastic strip thermometer stuck to the fermenter will help you keep an eye on the temperature. If you cannot find a place where temperatures are optimal and constant, don't panic. Just try to get the temperature in the proper range, and things will probably work out fine. You can always drape the fermenter with an electric blanket at night if it threatens to get too cold.

If you are making an ale, you should see yeast activity within 24 hours. Bubbles escaping from the fermentation lock will tell you how the yeast is doing. Once the yeast is up and running, fermentation should proceed quickly, with several bubbles escaping from the lock each second. At optimal temperatures an ale yeast will ordinarily go through its entire life cycle — *respiration*, reproduction, fermentation, and *flocculation* — in about a week. Soon thereafter the rate of bubble production will drop to one per second, and the rate will steadily lessen as more and more yeast organisms stop eating and drop out of solution. Eventually, all fermentation activity will stop. A hydrometer reading at this point will tell you if it is safe to bottle.

14. Bottle and cap.

HOW TO USE THE HYDROMETER

The hydrometer is a graduated glass instrument that measures the density, or "specific gravity," of liquids as compared to water. (Note: Specific gravity may be abbreviated as "S.G." or simply referred to as "gravity.") The hydrometer that comes with the equipment set is likely to be very delicate and requires careful handling. The first one we had broke from temperature stress while being rinsed. Some of the more expensive models are more durable. Because the hydrometer never touches the potential beer, it does not need to be sanitized, but it should be kept clean. The plastic tube you use to take a hydrometer reading will need to be sanitized, however, unless you are using a wine thief or turkey baster to fill it (in which case you must sanitize them).

You ordinarily use the hydrometer twice in basic brewing: first to test the specific gravity of the unfermented wort (initial gravity), and second to find the gravity of the finished beer (final gravity). The initial reading is taken after the wort has been topped up to 5 gallons (19L) — but before the yeast is pitched — and gives the brewer an idea of the amount of fermentable material in the wort. The second reading is used to confirm that fermentation is complete. Because alcohol is less dense than water, the final gravity reading will always be less than the initial gravity reading. A hydrometer reading that is higher than it ought to be indicates that fermentation may not be complete.

To take a reading, fill the plastic hydrometer case with wort to about ½ inch (1 cm) from the top. Place the hydrometer in the wort and gently spin it with your fingers to remove air bubbles. Find where the liquid crosses the scale in the neck of the hydrometer, and write down this figure. When reading a hydrometer, you should sight directly across the top of the liquid to get a true reading.

The density of pure water is considered to be 1.000 at 59°F (15°C). You will probably be measuring liquids that are much warmer, in the 70° to 90°F (21°–32°C) range, so you need to make an adjustment, or correction, of about .001 for every 10 degrees F (6 degrees C) greater than 59°F (15°C). For instance, if the wort measures 1.035 at 90°F (21°C), then add .003 to 1.035 for an initial gravity reading of 1.038.

After taking the reading, pour the wort sample down the sink. If you return the sample to the fermenter, you could contaminate the beer.

When you feel that fermentation is complete, that is, in about 7 days or when there are no more fermentation bubbles, take another reading. If it falls within the range given in the recipe, you can safely bottle the beer. If not, wait a week and take another reading. If that reading falls within the given range, proceed with bottling. If it is unchanged or remains high, then the fermentation may be finished. It could also be "stuck" (see Chapter 6: Troubleshooting).

Assuming that the beer is finished, you can now determine how much alcohol is in it. When using the hydrometer's potential alcohol scale, simply subtract the final gravity reading on the scale from the initial gravity reading. You can also subtract the final gravity from the initial gravity, and multiply by 105 to get the percent of alcohol by weight. The alcohol content of homebrew varies from 3 percent in low-alcohol brews to 10 or 11 percent in a serious brew.

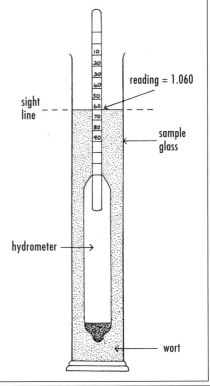

BREWING WITH KITS: A CHECKLIST

1. Sanitize the plastic fermenting bucket, lid, long-handled spoon, fermentation lock, strainer, thermometer, plastic tube, and hydrometer in a weak solution of water and household bleach (about one capful to the gallon). ❑

2. Add 1½ gallons (6L) of cold water to your fermenting bucket and chill. ❑

3. Remove the label from the malt extract can and immerse the can unopened in warm water. ❑

4. Bring 1½ gallons (6L) of water to a boil in the brew pot. Also, bring ½ gallon (2L) of hop rinsing water to a boil in a saucepan. ❑

5. Add malt extract to the brew pot and begin boiling for 20 minutes. ❑

6. After 15 minutes of boiling, add hops to the wort and continue boiling for another 5 minutes (total boil time: 20 minutes). ❑

7. Pour boiled wort through the strainer into fermenter. ❑

8. Rinse the hops with boiled water from the saucepan. ❑

9. Add enough cold water to the fermenter to make up 5 gallons (19L). ❑

10. Take a hydrometer reading and write it down. ❑

11. When wort has cooled to 75°F (24°C), pitch (add) yeast. ❑

12. Attach the fermentation lock and cover. ❑

13. Ferment for 7 to 10 days. ❑

14. Bottle and cap. ❑

BOTTLING YOUR BEER

Once the beer is finished, it can be bottled. This chore goes a lot faster if two people are involved, one to fill the bottles and one to cap. From setup to clean up, bottling usually takes only an hour or so.

Bottling Equipment

- ◆ **Fifty empty solid-neck beer bottles.** These are the kind of bottles for which you need an opener. No twist-offs here. They should be brown or green, but never clear. Sunlight is bad for beer. Bottles are available very cheaply from bottle redemption and distribution centers, or you can collect your own. A last resort is your homebrew store, which may have cheap used bottles instead of the expensive new ones. We like to use 28-ounce (820 ml) glass soda bottles that we get from a local bottling works, and we recycle any large microbrew bottles and swing-type Grolsch bottles that come our way. (Grolsch bottles used to have porcelain tops, but these were nonrecyclable, so they went to plastic. Their rubber gaskets will last a long time, and replacements can be had at your homebrew store.)

- ◆ **Five 5-gallon (19L) food-grade plastic buckets** for soaking bottles. These are available cheaply from anyone who handles food in bulk. It is a good idea to know what was in the buckets; foods like jelly or pickles can leave residues that are bad for beer. We got ours from Dunkin' Donuts for about a buck each.

- ◆ **Plastic bottling bucket with spigot.** This is the smaller of the two buckets that came with the equipment set.

- ◆ **Plastic tubing.** A short length of ½-inch (1-cm) tubing comes with the equipment set. You may find that a longer one is easier to use.

- ◆ **Filler wand.** A plastic tube with a spring valve at one end, which usually comes with the equipment set. These are not very rugged but will be adequate for your first few batches of beer. Later you will want to invest in a better one. These are available at your homebrew store.

- ◆ **Capper.** The capper that comes with the equipment set is fine. We have been using ours for several years now.

- ◆ **Three saucepans.** You will need these to prepare priming solution and gelatin and to sanitize bottle caps.

- ◆ **¾ cup (180 ml) of corn sugar** for priming the beer.

- ◆ **Unflavored gelatin** for fining.

- ◆ **Bottle caps.**

- ◆ **Long-handled spoon.**

Bottling: The Steps in Detail

This section gives a detailed description of how to bottle your homebrew. You'll find a quick-reference checklist summarizing these same steps in a box on page 27.

1. Sanitize the bottles in a weak solution of household bleach. Mix up the sanitizing solution in the 5-gallon (19L) buckets. Leave the bottles in the sanitizing solution for a few days. If they have labels, this will soak them off. The glue on these labels varies from company to company; some labels come off with a little soaking, and some never want to let go. Stubborn labels can be removed with a scouring pad. If the bottles are dirty to begin with (as bottles from the distribution center usually are), you will probably want to repeat this process to make sure you get them really clean. Do not clean homebrew bottles with detergent! Soapy residues are very bad for your beer. If a bottle is so scummy that it must be cleaned with soap, do your beer and the earth a favor: Recycle it and get another bottle. Rinsing out bottles immediately after pouring a beer makes cleaning them much easier.

2. Sanitize the bottling bucket (secondary fermenter), plastic tubing, filler wand, capper, and spoon. On the day you plan to bottle the beer, mix up sanitizing solution in the bottling bucket and sanitize your equipment. Let it soak for at least 30 minutes.

3. Siphon the beer from the primary fermenter into the bottling bucket. Arrange the primary fermenter so that it is higher than the secondary. Have a container ready to catch the siphoning water. Fill the sanitized plastic tubing completely with water, using your thumbs to seal the ends of the tube. Now, while

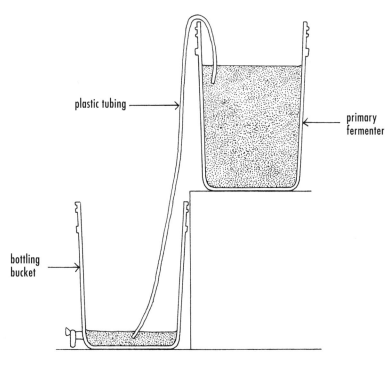

plastic tubing

primary fermenter

bottling bucket

Siphoning

holding your thumb over one end, put the other end of the tube into the primary fermenter. Hold the free end over the container, remove your thumb from the end, and let the clear water flow out into the container. When the beer starts to flow out (you can tell when this happens by the color change), stop it with your thumb. Then place the free end into the bottling bucket and remove your thumb. Carefully siphon your beer into the bottling bucket. Try to avoid sucking up sediment from the bottom of the primary. Hint: As the beer level gets very low, tip the primary up on its side to get the last of it.

4. Boil ¾ of a cup (180 ml) of corn sugar with 2 cups (470 ml) of water for priming. Boil the priming solution in the first saucepan. Stir it to keep it from burning. Priming sugar helps to carbonate beer by giving the yeast an extra bit of food to digest while it is in the bottle. This produces carbon dioxide, which remains in solution in the beer until you open it. Then it foams up, creating the head and bubbles.

5. Put bottle caps in the second saucepan, cover with cold water, and boil for 5 minutes. This sterilizes the caps. Strain them into a sanitized colander.

6. Heat one packet of unflavored gelatin with 2 cups (470 ml) of water in the third saucepan. Do not boil. Heat the mixture to 110°F (43°C). Gelatin is a fining, or clarifying, agent that will remove small particles of protein and yeast residues from the beer. Boiled gelatin cannot react with the particles and is useless as a fining agent.

7. Add sugar solution and gelatin solution to the beer. Stir with a sanitized spoon.

8. Rinse out bottles with hot water. Rinsing with hot water removes the bleach, preventing it from killing the yeast. Later you may want to invest in a bottle washer, but for now you do not need one.

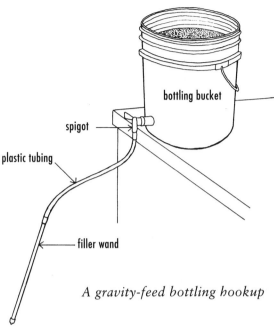

A gravity-feed bottling hookup

9. Sanitize bottling-bucket spigot. Rinse the bottling-bucket spigot with a small amount of sanitizing solution in a measuring cup or similar container. Rinse again with hot water.

10. Attach plastic tubing and filler wand. Arrange the bottling bucket above your work space so that gravity will drain the fermenter. Attach plastic tubing to the bottling-bucket spigot. Assemble sanitized filler wand and attach it to the plastic tubing. Open the spigot.

11. Fill the bottles. Press the filler wand against the bottom of the bottle to release the beer. Lift it up to shut off the flow. Leave approximately 1 inch (2½ cm) of headspace in your bottles. With less, it

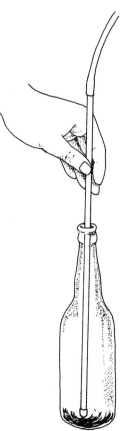

Filling a bottle

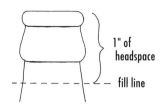

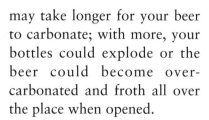

Proper headspace

may take longer for your beer to carbonate; with more, your bottles could explode or the beer could become over-carbonated and froth all over the place when opened.

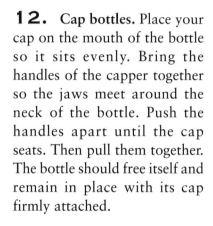

Capping

1 2. **Cap bottles.** Place your cap on the mouth of the bottle so it sits evenly. Bring the handles of the capper together so the jaws meet around the neck of the bottle. Push the handles apart until the cap seats. Then pull them together. The bottle should free itself and remain in place with its cap firmly attached.

1 3. **Label.** There is no need for an elaborate label; you only need to be able to identify the beer. Someday there will be more than one kind of beer in your beer cellar. We generally just write the initials of the beer's name and date of bottling on the bottle cap with a permanent marker. If you desire labels, you can buy them at the brew store or make them yourself. Some people use a computer to make fancy labels. Homemade labels can be stuck to the bottles with milk; they will stay in place and are easy to wash off.

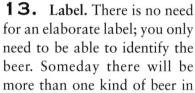

Bottle with label

1 4. **Store and age.** Beer stores best in a cool, dark place such as a cellar. Cardboard

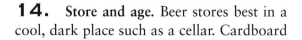

case boxes work well for this purpose, and most homebrew batches will make two cases of beer. Beer must be aged to allow natural carbonation to take place. Some flavors will change subtly with aging. Ales generally will be ready to drink in 2–6 weeks. Lagers should be aged for at least 1–2 months.

BOTTLING BEER: A CHECKLIST

1. Sanitize the bottles in a weak solution of household bleach. ❏
2. Sanitize the bottling bucket, plastic tubing, filler wand, capper, and spoon. ❏
3. Siphon the beer from the primary fermenter into the bottling bucket. ❏
4. Boil ¾ cup (180 ml) of corn sugar with 2 cups (470 ml) of water in a saucepan. ❏
5. Put bottle caps in a second saucepan, cover with cold water, and boil for 5 minutes. ❏
6. Heat 1 packet of unflavored gelatin with 2 cups (470 ml) of water in a third saucepan. Do not boil. ❏
7. Add sugar solution and gelatin solution to the beer. Stir with a sanitized spoon. ❏
8. Rinse out bottles with hot water. ❏
9. Sanitize bottling-bucket spigot. ❏
10. Attach plastic tubing and filler wand. ❏
11. Fill the bottles. ❏
12. Cap the bottles. ❏
13. Label. ❏
14. Store and age. ❏

2

SELECTING THE RIGHT INGREDIENTS

THERE IS A REAL SHORTAGE of information available to the homebrewer on kits, and that's one of the reasons we wrote this book. Most of the time, the manufacturers provide only a bare description of what's in their kits — malt extract, hop extract, and yeast — without telling you what kind of malts and hops were used and in what amounts. While most kit producers are scrupulous, it's also a sad fact that some of them adulterate their products with corn sugar even while claiming that they are "all malt." Corn sugar is cheaper than malt extract but makes for a thin, cidery brew. So never add sugar to a kit because there may already be some in the extract.

Most kit manufacturers are very secretive about their ingredients, and this is too bad. It means that the homebrewer has to work in a cloud of ignorance about what's in the can. Sooner or later, better labeling standards will have to come about. There has been some movement in that direction already, especially among American microbrewers who are producing their own kits. In the meantime, experimentation is the only way to find out if a particular kit suits your needs. If you find a kit you like, keep using it.

Distributors have a lot of information about the products they sell, and there is no law against your calling them and asking for it, or asking your brew store people to do it for you. If enough people ask, this information may become more readily available.

SECRETS OF THE CAN

Pay attention to the date on any can of malt extract. It's not immortal and should be used within a few years of manufacture. Age affects certain characteristics of malt extract more than others. For instance, extract darkens as it gets older, which is not much of a problem if you are making a stout, but it can affect the color of a lighter beer.

Our friends at Stout Billy's have also noticed significant color differences between batches of malt extract from the most reliable companies, so don't be surprised if there is some variation from can to can. While color may be the least important factor in the ordinary enjoyment of beer, it is nice to have a beer that looks the way it is supposed to.

Some other things you should know about kits:

Weight. Most can kit companies use a standard weight for all their products regardless of style. Laaglander's kits are available in both 3.3- and 4-pound (1.5- and 1.8-kg) sizes; Ironmaster and Mountmellick both use a standard 4 pounds (1.8 kg). John Bull and Edme both have standard kits weighing in at 3.3 pounds (1.5 kg), and their special and "premium" kits weigh 4 pounds (1.8 kg). Geordie just increased the size of their basic kits from 3.3 to 3.5 pounds (1.5 to 1.6 kg). Some companies such as Black Rock use a slightly heavier can for their higher-gravity beers. Knowing the weight of the can is especially useful when you begin formulating your own recipes.

Starting specific gravity. All starting specific gravities are estimated for one can of malt extract dissolved in 5 U.S. gallons (19L) of water. This information gives you an idea of the exact amount of fermentable material contributed by the malt. Knowing this allows you to determine the strength of the finished beer, and it gives you a starting point when designing your own recipes.

Some kits have an estimate of original specific gravity (O.G.) printed on the label. Generally, it's not a good idea to use these figures to estimate the potential strength of your brew because they are not calculated using U.S. gallons. British companies use Imperial gallons (1.2 U.S. gallons), and European companies may even use liters (3.785 per U.S. gallon).

Sometimes the specific gravities listed on the label are calculated to include extra sugar, not just the malt extract in the can. This assumes that the homebrewer is following the instructions included with the kit. If you follow our advice and don't add sugar, you will get a lower specific gravity than the one given by the manufacturer.

HBU per can. Wherever possible, we have included the HBUs (Homebrew Bitterness Units) for each kit. HBUs, a measure of bitterness potential for a given volume of beer, are derived from the amount of hops used multiplied by the percent of alpha acid. Hop bitterness in kits usually comes from the use of hop extract. Ordinary hop extract must be boiled for some time to realize its bittering potential. Some kits list "iso-hop" extract as an ingredient. This is a form of hop extract that has been altered on a molecular level to produce bitterness immediately.

Ingredients. These are the ingredients listed on the label or given out in the manufacturers' specifications. The bulk of any kit is, or should be, barley malt extract or some other form of malt, such as wheat. Some manufacturers also add a variety of *adjuncts,* such as rice extract and corn syrup. Glycerine and d-glucitol are used to enhance body. Caramelized sugar may be added as a coloring agent. Brewferm's specialty kits include fruit juices and herbs. In addition to hop extracts, a few companies also add whole hops to their kits.

KIT MANUFACTURERS AND THEIR PRODUCTS

The following are by no means all of the available kits. There are hundreds of them, and there isn't room or reason to include everything on the market. These are kits we have had success with and which are available around the country. Most of them are used in one or more of our recipes. New products are always appearing, and we have included some of the most interesting new kits here.

Black Rock

A brand-new entry from New Zealand, Black Rock is becoming a big producer of kits. The company makes ten different European- and English-style kits from native barley and hops. We've had good luck with their products and yeasts.

> *Black Rock Bock.* Weight: 3.75 pounds (1.7 kg). Starting specific gravity: 1.025. New Zealand 2-row barley malt extract, Motueka hops.
>
> *Black Rock East India Pale Ale.* Weight: 3.3 pounds (1.5 kg). Starting specific gravity: 1.026. New Zealand 2-row barley malt extract, Motueka hops.
>
> *Black Rock Miner's Stout.* Weight: 3.75 pounds (1.7 kg). Starting specific gravity: 1.029. New Zealand 2-row barley malt extract, Motueka hops.

Brewferm

This Belgian company produces versions of many traditional and unusual Belgian beer styles. Some of the wildest and weirdest of the world's brews come from this tiny nation. Many of them are not much like our idea of beer at all; they're more like fine and potent wines.

> *Brewferm Abbey.* Weight: 3.3 pounds (1.5 kg). Starting specific gravity: 1.035. Continental 2-row barley malt extract, hop

extract. Strong, dark, reddish-brown ale with good keeping quality. Full-flavored taste, malty aroma. Thick, lacy, long-lasting head.

Brewferm Amiorix. Weight: 3.3 pounds (1.5 kg). Starting specific gravity: 1.036. Continental 2-row barley malt extract, hop extract. Amber ale with reddish copper tint. Slightly acidic palate with sweet aftertaste.

Brewferm Christmas. Weight: 3.3 pounds (1.5 kg). Starting specific gravity: 1.025. Continental 2-row barley malt extract, hop extract. Dark, strong, full-bodied Belgian ale, sweeter than Abbey-style beers. Strong malt flavor and aroma. Christmas-style ales have good keeping quality and get better and better with age. Extraordinary head retention.

Brewferm Diabolo. Weight: 3.3 pounds (1.5 kg). Starting specific gravity: 1.031. Continental 2-row barley malt extract, hop extract. Golden ale with a thick, lacy head. Soft palate and characteristic aroma of Devil-type Belgian ales. Also compares with Belgian Tripel ales.

Brewferm Framboise. Weight: 3.3 pounds (1.5 kg). Starting specific gravity: 1.035. Continental 2-row barley malt extract, raspberry juice, glycerine, hop extract. Apart from Brewferm Kriek, the only other fruit beer kit in the world. No artificial flavors. Each can contains the juice of 4.4 pounds (2 kg) of raspberries. Delicate aroma.

Brewferm Grand Cru. Weight: 3.3 pounds (1.5 kg). Starting specific gravity: 1.034. Continental 2-row barley malt extract, wheat extract, oat flakes, herbs, hop extract. Opalescent gold color, strong malty flavor. Some hop aroma, full body, fruity flavor, sweet aftertaste.

Brewferm King. Weight: 3.3 pounds (1.5 kg). Starting specific gravity for 5 gallons (19L): 1.034. Continental 2-row barley malt extract, hop extract. Sweet amber dessert beer, lighter colored than Abbey, with vinous character.

Brewferm Kriek. Weight: 3.3 pounds (1.5 kg). Starting specific gravity: 1.035. Continental 2-row barley malt extract, cherry juice, glycerine, citric acid, hop extract. Some cherry aroma, low cherry flavor, slightly acidic, low bitterness, full body. Red tint. Each can contains the juice of 6.6 pounds (3 kg) of cherries.

Brewferm Old Flemish Brown. Weight: 3.3 pounds (1.5 kg). Starting specific gravity: 1.040. Continental 2-row barley malt extract, hop extract. Dark brown ale with red tint and slight licorice aftertaste. Compares with Dutch Bock beers. Belgian Flanders Brown is a strong aromatic beer with good keeping quality.

Brewferm Pilsner. Weight: 3.3 pounds (1.5 kg). Starting specific gravity: 1.028. Continental 2-row barley malt extract, hop extract. Light-blond beer, comparable with commercial lager beers.

Brewferm Scotch. Weight: 3.3 pounds (1.5 kg). Starting specific gravity: 1.024. Continental 2-row barley malt extract, hop extract. Comparable to traditional Scotch ales. Halfway between Christmas and Abbey. Malty and full-bodied, with good keeping quality.

Brewferm Tripel. Weight: 3.3 pounds (1.5 kg). Starting specific gravity: 1.034. Continental 2-row barley malt extract, herbs, hop extract. Deep golden, full-bodied, strong ale. Malty aroma and taste.

Brewferm Wheat. Weight: 3.3 pounds (1.5 kg). Starting specific gravity: 1.042. Continental 2-row barley malt extract, wheat extract, hop extract. Comparable to Belgian Witbier, very pale honey color, low alcohol, sweet aroma, slightly acid taste.

Cooper's

Made in Leabrook, South Australia, Cooper's kits are reliable and popular.

Cooper's Bitter. Weight: 3.3 pounds (1.5 kg). Starting specific gravity: 1.025. Australian 2-row barley malt extract, hop extract. Grainy aroma and flavor, caramel and roasted notes. Mild bitterness, medium body.

Cooper's Draught. Weight: 3.3 pounds (1.5 kg). Starting specific gravity: 1.025. Australian 2-row barley malt extract, hop extract. Golden and smooth.

Cooper's Lager. Weight 3.3 pounds (1.5 kg). Starting specific gravity: 1.022. Australian 2-row barley malt extract, hop extract. Light-straw color with a shot of hops. Typical of the thirst-quenching and robust Australian lagers.

Cooper's Real Ale. Weight: 3.3 pounds (1.5 kg). Starting specific gravity: 1.025. Australian 2-row barley malt extract, hop extract. Hoppy aroma, nice bitterness, medium body.

Cooper's Stout. Weight 3.3 pounds (1.5 kg). Starting specific gravity: 1.025. Australian 2-row barley malt extract, hop extract. Smooth and dark, but not too heavy.

Geordie

Geordie kits are produced by Wander Ltd. of Hertshire, England.

Geordie American Light. Weight: 3.5 pounds (1.6 kg). Starting specific gravity: 1.020. HBU per can: 1.5. English 2-row barley malt extract, caramel, hop extract.

Geordie Bitter. Weight: 3.5 pounds (1.6 kg). Starting specific gravity: 1.022. HBU per can: 3.4. English 2-row barley malt extract, caramel, hop extract.

Geordie Lager. Weight: 3.5 pounds (1.6 kg). Starting specific gravity: 1.020. HBU per can: 0.9. English 2-row barley malt extract, caramel, hop extract.

Geordie Mild. Weight: 3.5 pounds (1.6 kg). Starting specific gravity: 1.025. HBU per can: 2.7. English 2-row barley malt extract, roasted barley extract, caramel, hop extract. Dark, with the fuller Northern taste.

Geordie Scottish Export. Weight: 3.5 pounds (1.6 kg). Starting specific gravity: 1.025. HBU per can: 3.0. English 2-row barley malt extract, caramel, hop extract. Produces the rounded taste and distinctive aroma of Scottish ales.

Geordie Yorkshire Bitter. Weight: 3.5 pounds (1.6 kg). Starting specific gravity: 1.025. English 2-row barley malt extract, caramel, hop extract, calcium chloride.

Glen Brew

Glen Brew kits are produced by Glen Brew Ltd. of Kirkliston, Scotland.

Glen Brew Bavarian Pilsner. Weight: 6.6 pounds (3 kg). Starting specific gravity: 1.052. Continental 2-row barley malt extract, hop extract.

Glen Brew Chairman's Trophy Bitter. Weight: 6.6 pounds (3 kg). Starting specific gravity: 1.054. English 2-row barley malt extract, hop extract. Deep amber, pronounced hop bite and aroma. Caramelized malt aroma.

Glen Brew Dortmunder Export. Weight: 6.6 pounds (3 kg). Starting specific gravity: 1.052. Continental 2-row barley malt extract, hop extract.

Glen Brew Irish Stout. Weight: 6.6 pounds (3 kg). Starting specific gravity: 1.054. English 2-row barley malt extract, crystal malt extract, roasted barley extract, iso-hop extract. Dry Irish-style stout, with some tannic notes.

Ironmaster

Brewing Products Ltd. of Kirkliston, Scotland, makes Ironmaster as well as Telford's kits.

Ironmaster British Special Bitter. Weight: 4 pounds (1.8 kg). Starting specific gravity: 1.029. HBU per can: 18.0. English 2-row barley malt extract, crystal malt extract, hop extract, iso-hop extract.

Ironmaster Imperial Pale Ale. Weight: 4 pounds (1.8 kg). Starting specific gravity: 1.032. HBU per can: 14.0. English 2-row barley malt extract, hop extract.

Ironmaster Northern Brown Ale. Weight: 4 pounds (1.8 kg). Starting specific gravity: 1.029. HBU per can: 12.8. English 2-row barley malt extract, crystal malt extract, hop extract.

Ironmaster Old English Porter. Weight: 4 pounds (1.8 kg). Starting specific gravity: 1.030. English 2-row barley malt extract, black malt extract, roasted barley extract, hop extract.

Ironmaster Scottish Mild. Weight: 4 pounds (1.8 kg). Starting specific gravity: 1.030. HBU per can: 14.0. English 2-row barley malt extract, hop extract.

Ironmaster Special Export Bitter. Weight: 4 pounds (1.8 kg). Starting specific gravity: 1.032. HBU per can: 18.0. English 2-row barley malt extract, hop extract.

Ironmaster Special Lager. Weight: 4 pounds (1.8 kg). Starting specific gravity: 1.029. HBU per can: 16.0. English 2-row barley malt extract, hop extract.

Ironmaster Special Stout. Weight: 4 pounds (1.8 kg). Starting specific gravity: 1.030. HBU per can: 19.2. English 2-row barley malt extract, hop extract.

John Bull

Paine's Malt Ltd. of Huntingdon, England, maker of John Bull, produces some of the most reliable and popular kits in a wide variety of styles.

John Bull Amber Hopped. Weight: 3.3 pounds (1.5 kg). Starting specific gravity: 1.024. HBU per can: 10.0. English 2-row barley malt extract, hop extract.

John Bull American Beer. Weight: 3.3 pounds (1.5 kg). Starting specific gravity: 1.020. HBU per can: 4.5. English 2-row barley malt extract, hop extract.

John Bull American Light. Weight: 3.3 pounds (1.5 kg). Starting specific gravity: 1.020. HBU per can: 5.3. English 2-row barley malt extract, hop extract.

John Bull Canadian Beer. Weight: 3.3 pounds (1.5 kg). Starting specific gravity: 1.025. English 2-row barley malt extract, corn syrup, hops, iso-hop extract.

John Bull Light Hopped. Weight: 3.3 pounds (1.5 kg). Starting specific gravity: 1.020. HBU per can: 9.0. English 2-row barley malt extract, hop extract.

John Bull Master Class Bitter. Weight: 6.6 pounds (3 kg). Starting specific gravity: 1.042. HBU per can: 18.0. English 2-row barley malt extract, iso-hop extract, coloring, caramel, pelletized Kent hops, glucose, Irish moss, sodium bicarbonate.

John Bull Master Class Lager. (The Master Class are two-can kits. They are hard to find and a bit pricey for what you get.) Weight: 6.6 pounds (3 kg). Starting specific gravity: 1.040. HBU per can: 13.5. English 2-row barley malt extract, iso-hop extract, coloring, caramel, pelletized Hallertau hops, glucose, Irish moss, sodium bicarbonate.

Laaglander

A Dutch subsidiary of Paine's Malt Ltd., the producer of John Bull, Laaglander produces a popular line of can kits in various European styles.

Laaglander Irish Ale. Weight: 4 pounds (1.8 kg). Starting specific gravity: 1.030. HBU per can: 9.0. Continental 2-row barley malt extract, caramel, hop extract.

Laaglander Irish Stout. Weight: 4 pounds (1.8 kg). Starting specific gravity: 1.032. HBU per can: 15.0. Continental 2-row barley malt extract, malted barley, caramel, hop extract.

Laaglander Dutch Dark Lager. Weight: 4 pounds (1.8 kg). Starting specific gravity: 1.030. HBU per can: 6.0. Continental 2-row barley malt extract, roasted barley, caramel, hop extract.

Laaglander Dutch Light Lager. Weight: 4 pounds (1.8 kg). Starting specific gravity: 1.030. HBU per can: 10.5. Continental 2-row barley malt extract, hop extract.

Laaglander Traditional Strong Ale. Weight: 4 pounds (1.8 kg). Starting specific gravity: 1.032. HBU per can: 10.5. Continental 2-row barley malt extract, roasted barley, caramel, hops, iso-hop extract.

Mountmellick

Mountmellick of County Laois, Ireland, produces a popular line of all-malt kits from Irish 2-row barley. They get high marks from us for being one of the very few manufacturers that actually recommend the addition of aromatic hops to the boil.

Mountmellick Brown Ale. Weight: 4 pounds (1.8 kg). Starting specific gravity: 1.030. Irish 2-row barley malt extract, hop extract. Dark, silky, and hoppy.

Mountmellick Export Ale. Weight: 4 pounds (1.8 kg). Starting specific gravity: 1.032. Irish 2-row barley malt extract, hop extract. A classic amber ale.

Mountmellick Famous Irish Stout. Weight: 4 pounds (1.8 kg). Starting specific gravity: 1.032. Irish 2-row barley malt extract, roasted barley extract, hop extract, iso-hop extract. Dark and rich.

Munton & Fison

Munton & Fison of Stowmarket, Suffolk, England, produces dry extracts, hopped and plain extract syrups, and ale yeast as well as kits. Their products show up in a lot of award-winning recipes.

Munton & Fison American Light. Weight: 3.3 pounds (1.5 kg). Starting specific gravity: 1.020. HBU per can: 5.75. English 2-row barley malt extract, glucose syrup, hop extract. Lightly hopped.

Munton & Fison Old Ale. Weight: 3.3 pounds (1.5 kg). Starting specific gravity: 1.030. HBU per can: 12.5. English 2-row barley malt extract, d-glucitol, hop extract. Rich in body and flavor, strong, and dark.

Munton & Fison Pilsner. Weight: 3.3 pounds (1.5 kg). Starting specific gravity: 1.022. HBU per can: 7.5. English 2-row barley malt extract, hop extract. Light, full-bodied lager.

Munton & Fison Premium. Weight: 3.3 pounds (1.5 kg). Starting specific gravity: 1.025. HBU per can: 12.5. English 2-row barley malt extract, hop extract. Typical of traditional English ale.

Munton & Fison Stout. Weight: 3.3 pounds (1.5 kg). Starting specific gravity: 1.030. HBU per can: 13.75. English 2-row barley malt extract, hop extract. Rich, very dark, and very hoppy.

Premier

A Canadian-U.S. company with branches in both countries, Premier produces its malt extract kits in Canada. Their American division is in Grosse Pointe, Michigan.

> *Premier American Rice.* Weight: 3.3 pounds (1.5 kg). Starting specific gravity: 1.020. Barley malt extract, hop extract, rice extract, corn extract. Light, medium-bodied. A thirst-quencher.
>
> *Premier Wheat.* Weight: 3.3 pounds (1.5 kg). Starting specific gravity: 1.025. Wheat extract, barley extract, hop extract. Cloudy and tangy.

Telford's

Telford's uses real hops rather than just hop extracts in their kits. Telford's kits are produced by Brewing Products Ltd. of Kirkliston, Scotland.

> *Telford's Brown Ale.* Weight: 4 pounds (1.8 kg). Starting specific gravity: 1.024. British 2-row barley malt extract, crystal malt extract, hops, hop extract.
>
> *Telford's Gaelic Stout.* Weight: 4 pounds (1.8 kg). Starting specific gravity: 1.026. British 2-row barley malt extract, black malt extract, roasted barley, hops, hop extract.
>
> *Telford's Mild.* Weight: 4 pounds (1.8 kg). Starting specific gravity: 1.024. British 2-row barley malt extract, black malt extract, roasted barley, hops, hop extract.
>
> *Telford's Porter.* Weight: 4 pounds (1.8 kg). Starting specific gravity: 1.026. British 2-row barley malt extract, black malt extract, roasted barley, hops, hop extract. Roasted grain aroma, some dry tannic notes, full body. Little residual sweetness. Hoppy and grainy.
>
> *Telford's Premium Bitter.* Weight: 4 pounds (1.8 kg). Starting specific gravity: 1.025. British 2-row barley malt extract, crystal malt extract, hops, hop extract.

BREWING FOR EXCELLENCE

The addition of a few extra ingredients to the basic kit can work wonders for your beer, enhancing maltiness, hoppiness, and balance that may be missing from the basic kit. The small expense they add to kit brewing is more than compensated for by the improved quality of the finished product. A couple of pounds of malt grains, a few ounces of fragrant hops, and quality yeast will make the difference between making beer that is drinkable and beer that is truly excellent.

Malts

Specialty malts make a definite contribution to the brew, and since some of the recipes you will find in this book call for such malts, it's only fair that we explain what they are and how they are used.

In the list that follows, we have included the country of origin, the type of barley used, degrees *Lovibond* (a measurement of beer and grain color), a description, and recommended amounts to use in a 5-gallon (19L) batch of beer for each malt.

Pilsner malt. German 2-row, 1.5 degrees Lovibond. The basis for many European-style all-grain beers. ½ pound–1 pound (220–450 g).

Munich malt. German 2-row, 5.7 degrees Lovibond. Contributes malty flavor and orange color. ¼ pound–1 pound (110–450 g).

Cara-Pils malt. British 2-row, 10 degrees Lovibond. Contributes to body and head retention. ¼ pound–½ pound (110–220 g).

Aromatic malt. Belgian 2-row, 25 degrees Lovibond. A darker version of Munich malt. Adds malty aroma and taste, and a garnet color. ¼ pound–¾ pound (110–340 g).

Biscuit malt. Belgian 2-row, 27 degrees Lovibond. Adds a nutty, oatmeal biscuit flavor to beer. ¼ pound–¾ pound (110–340 g).

WATER, WATER EVERYWHERE

The best water for homebrew is soft and relatively free of chemicals such as chlorine. But if your tap water tastes good and smells good, then it is probably fine to use for kit brewing. It's really only when you get into all-grain brewing that water quality becomes crucial. If your home water is not up to brewing, you can probably find a source of springwater at some reasonable distance. If you can't, then the only alternative is to buy bottled water.

One problem that occurs with modern municipal water is that it often contains chlorine — so much chlorine that it can kill your yeast. If this happens to you, there are one or two things you can do: (1) Boil the water you plan to use in brewing (all 5 gallons, or 19L) before you start, then stir vigorously to aerate it; or (2) let your brewing water sit overnight to drive off the worst of the chlorine.

In the old days, beer was frequently substituted for drinking water because the local water supplies were foul. Converting water to beer destroys the evil microbes lurking in it because nothing bad can live in beer. During the reign of Elizabeth I, the beer ration for every man, woman, and child in England was a gallon per day! Good Queen Bess herself started every day by drinking two large bumpers of beer.

Special Roast malt. U.S. 2-row, 45 degrees Lovibond. Contributes body, roasted malt flavor, and deep orange color. ¼ pound–¾ pound (110–340 g).

Cara-Munich malt. Belgian 2-row, 70 degrees Lovibond. Contributes body, assertive malt taste, and a deep amber color. ¼ pound–1½ pounds (110 g–.7 kg).

Crystal malt. U.S., German, or British 2-row. The most commonly used variety is British 2-row, 60 degrees Lovibond, but this malt can range from 20–90 degrees

Lovibond. This is a "green" malt, one that has been kilned while wet. The process allows caramelization to take place inside the grains, contributing additional sweetness, body, and a golden or reddish color to the beer. Cara and caramel malts are also prepared this way. ¼ pound–1½ pounds (110 g–.7 kg).

Special B malt. Belgian 2-row, 200 degrees Lovibond. Between dark crystal and chocolate; most like a brown malt. Used in Belgian specialty ales. 2 ounces – ½ pound (57–220g).

Chocolate malt. British 2-row, 400 degrees Lovibond. A dark brown malt that has been roasted longer than crystal malt but not as long as black patent malt. Imparts a nutty, toasted flavor to beer. 2 ounces – ¾ pound (57–340 g).

Roasted Barley. British 2-row, 500 degrees Lovibond. A rich, dark brown grain made from unmalted barley. Used especially in stout, where it contributes a roasted flavor, bitterness, and a brown head. A small amount of roasted barley contributes a dark red color to lighter beers. 2 ounces– 1 pound (57–450 g).

Black Patent malt. British 2-row, 530 degrees Lovibond. Roasted malted barley that has had all its flavor driven off. Mostly used for coloring beer. Colors the beer's head, but not as much as roasted barley, and contributes a dry, burnt bitterness unlike that of hops. 2 ounces–¾ pound (57–340 g).

Hops

Hops, the female flowers of the vine *Humulus lupulus,* are a fairly recent addition to beer, having only been used regularly in brewing since the 16th century. Originally, hops not only provided bitterness and aroma to beer but also helped to preserve it. That's still part of their function. But today, because flavor and aroma are so important to the enjoyment of beer, and because hops are sometimes too fragile to survive canning, you may want to add hops to kit brews. Even a half-ounce of aroma hops added at the end of the boil can make a world of difference to the quality of your beer.

Hops are generally available to the homebrewer in three forms: loose, plugs, and pellets. Loose hops are whole hop flowers that come in 1- or 4-ounce (28–110 g) bags. Hop plugs are whole hops that have been compressed into ½-ounce (14 g) cakes that loosen up in the boil. Pelletized hops are hops that have been pulverized and converted into pellets. They take up less space per ounce than loose or plug hops, but they are also more difficult to remove from the wort.

Hops are used mainly to provide a bitter flavor to balance the sweetness of malt. This is accomplished in a process called "bittering," in which bitter alpha and beta acids are extracted from hops during a long boil.

Kits are usually sufficiently bitter because the bittering acids survive the canning process very well. If you want to brew a style of beer that is characteristically bitter, it is best to add fresh bittering hops.

Hops can also be used to add a subtle herbal tang to the brew, with specific flavor depending on the variety of hops used. Some complex beers, such as bitters, may use two, or even three, different varieties of flavoring hops.

Aromatic or *finishing hops,* added during the final minutes of the boil, provide a delicately hoppy "nose" to the beer. Dry hopping, which is adding hops to the beer during *secondary fermentation,* can also add a very fresh hop aroma to the beer. Remember that a large part of your sense of taste is actually that of smell; so good beer aroma equals better taste.

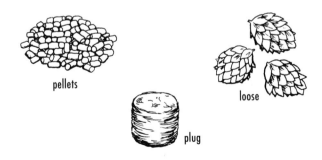

pellets

plug

loose

Three types of hops

Of course, different hops have different uses. Some are exclusively for bittering, flavoring, or finishing, and some hops are interchangeable, depending on when and in what amount they are added to the boil.

In the following list of hops, the first item is an estimate of the percentage of alpha acids, which gives you an idea of the bitterness potential of each hop — the higher alpha values indicating greater bitterness. The country of origin, a description, and uses come next.

We also note if a hop is considered "noble." This is a fairly arbitrary measurement of general quality and excellence of aroma that was determined 150 or 200 years ago in the Austro-Hungarian Empire. Noble hops are still with us, although the empire is not.

Cascade. 5–7 percent. U.S./Canada. Spicy floral aroma. Gives characteristic flavor to American lagers. Signature hop of American Pale ales. Uses: bittering, flavoring, aroma.

Chinook. 12–14 percent. U.S. Very bitter, with some aromatic qualities. Uses: bittering; some brewers use it for aroma, dry hopping.

East Kent Goldings. 5–7 percent. England. Delicate, subtly spicy hop. Classic British ale hop. Uses: bittering, flavoring, aroma.

Eroica. 10–13 percent. U.S. Very bitter, some aromatic qualities. Often used to bitter darker British ales.

Fuggles. 4–7 percent. England. Traditional British ale hop. Mild, earthy. Uses: bittering, flavoring, aroma.

Hallertau. 4–6 percent. Germany/U.S. Traditional lager hop. Noble when grown in Germany. Clean and floral. Uses: bittering, flavoring, aroma.

Liberty. 4–6 percent. U.S. Mild, pleasant, with subtle spiciness. Bred to resemble Hallertau. Uses: aroma, flavoring.

Northern Brewer. 7.5–9.5 percent. Germany/U.S./Belgium. Bold, bitter, aromatic. Uses: bittering, aroma.

Perle. 7–9 percent. U.S./Germany. Similar to Northern Brewer. Traditional German lager hop. Uses: bittering, flavoring, aroma.

Saaz. 4–6 percent. Czech Republic. Traditional Pilsner hop. Floral, elegant. Noble when grown in Czech Republic. Uses: bittering, flavoring, aroma.

Styrian Goldings. 5–7.5 percent. Slovenia (former Yugoslavia). Excellent ale hop. Aromatic, clean. Uses: bittering, flavoring, aroma.

Tettnang. 4–6 percent. U.S./Germany. American lager hop. Spicy and distinctive. Noble when grown in Germany. Uses: bittering, flavoring, aroma.

Willamette. 5–7.5 percent. U.S. Aromatic, developed as a slightly spicier, seedless American Fuggles. Uses: bittering, flavoring, aroma.

Yeast

Yeast is the heart of brewing. Without good active yeast, all your other ingredients cannot become beer. Brewer's yeast, as we have said elsewhere, comes in two basic types: top-fermenting ale yeast and bottom-fermenting lager yeast. *All yeast packets provided with kits contain ale yeast.* This was probably done to simplify the process and reduce fermentation time. However, a lager wort fermented with ale yeast is no longer lager; it's ale. Similarly, ale worts can be fermented with lager yeast at cool temperatures to produce acceptable lager beers.

Yeast Action

The life cycle of yeast can be divided into four stages: respiration, reproduction, fermentation, and flocculation. Respiration is the phase in which yeast absorbs oxygen that has been dissolved in the wort and begins eating in preparation for the next stage. In reproduction, the yeast reproduces asexually by means of budding. Each yeast cell produces hundreds of thousands of offspring, which in turn start respiring and reproducing. This is why the first stages of the fermentation process are so dramatic, resulting in billowing **kraeusen** and an enormous release of carbon dioxide (CO_2).

When a critical population of yeast organisms is reached, fermentation takes place. In this stage, yeast cells continue digesting sugars and producing carbon dioxide, but they also begin to produce alcohol. As the yeast organisms run out of food, flocculation occurs. During this stage, exhausted yeast cells prepare for dormancy and begin dropping out of solution, a process known as sedimentation. Lager yeasts sediment to the bottom of the fermenter; true ale yeasts rise to the top.

Eventually, all yeast, even top-fermenting varieties, will drop out of solution to the bottom of the fermenter. The beer is then said to have "dropped clear," and it may be bottled. The clearing process for ales can be speeded up by placing the fermenter in a cold room. Beer can also be cleared by adding a fining agent, such as gelatin or isinglass, to the fermenter.

Top-Fermenting and Bottom-Fermenting Yeasts

Top-fermenting yeasts, as noted above, accumulate at the top of the fermenter. They favor warm temperatures, act rapidly, and tend to produce *esters,* which are tasty organic compounds. The desirability of esters varies with beer style and the level of esters present. The use of top-fermenting yeast in ales accounts for their highly complex flavors.

Bottom-fermenting yeasts accumulate at the bottom of the fermenter. They act at lower temperatures than ale yeasts and over a much longer period of time. This tends to produce a beer with a clean, subtle flavor.

Both top- and bottom-fermenting yeasts are generally available in three forms: dried yeast, liquid yeast, and liquid yeast packets. Whatever form it's in, you need to keep it refrigerated until just before you're ready to brew. **Unrefrigerated yeast should never be used!** Old yeast is also suspect and should be watched to see if it starts. Of course, you can make your own yeast starter (see below).

Dried yeast comes in a packet just like bread yeast, is really easy to use, and is favored by beginners. Just rip it open and pour it into the fermenter. Unlike liquid yeast it takes off rapidly (within a few hours) and finishes rapidly; there isn't a lot of waiting around.

Dried yeast can also be hydrated for slightly faster results. Dissolve the yeast in a sanitized cup with ½ cup (125 ml) of warm (70° to 80°F, 21° to 27°C) water and allow to "proof" for 10–15 minutes before *pitching.* You can add a teaspoon of dried malt extract to the liquid if you want, but it's not really necessary.

Liquid yeast comes in a vial and can be used just as easily. Leave it at room temperature and shake it up before pitching. Liquid yeast packets — Wyeast, for example — contain a liquid yeast culture that is kept separate from a malt-extract food source in a plastic bag. To use the yeast, you have to break the plastic bag inside the envelope (without breaking the envelope) and allow the yeast to work in a warm place for three days or more, depending on the age of the packet. Old yeast takes longer. To

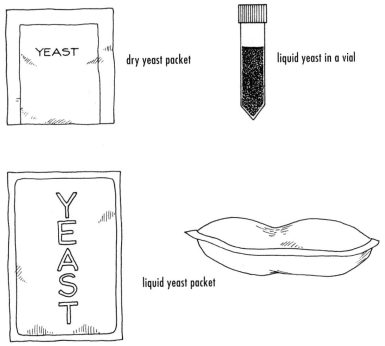

dry yeast packet

liquid yeast in a vial

liquid yeast packet

Three types of yeast

LIQUID VERSUS DRY YEAST

Dry yeast is cheap, highly reliable, easy to use, and nearly fool-proof. However, not every variety of yeast that a homebrewer will want to use is found in dry form. Liquid yeasts, on the other hand, are more expensive and can be temperamental, but they offer a wide range of yeast cultures and a high degree of quality. Liquid yeast packets take a little advance preparation, so you need to plan ahead when you brew. If you are a spur-of-the-moment brewer, you'll probably want to stick with dry.

One way of cutting down on the expense of liquid yeast is to culture it yourself. This way you can get several batches of brew out of a single packet of yeast. Yeast culturing is beyond the scope of this book, but you can find good information about it in Roger Leistad's *Yeast Culturing for the Homebrewer* (G.W. Kent, 1983).

It is fairly simple to make a liquid yeast starter, which will enable you to get your 5-gallon (19L) batch off to a quick start. You will need:

> 5 tablespoons of dry malt extract (75 ml)
> a sanitized funnel
> 1 sanitized 22-ounce beer bottle (650 ml)
> 1 sanitized cap
> #2 rubber stopper with airlock

Boil dry malt extract with 2 cups (470 ml) of water for 5 minutes. Pour the boiled wort into the sanitized beer bottle with a funnel and cap the bottle. Allow the wort to cool and then refrigerate it until you are ready to make beer. About 18 to 24 hours before brewing, shake the bottle vigorously to aerate the wort, uncap the bottle, and pitch with liquid yeast. Cork the bottle with a #2 stopper and airlock. Allow the bottle to sit in a warm place (70° to 80°F, 21° to 27°C) until ready to pitch.

break the bag, place the packet on a flat surface and smack it soundly with your hand. Wyeast packets must be allowed to work for 3 to 7 days (again, depending on the age of the packet) before pitching. Leave the packet undisturbed in a warm place. The yeast will begin to eat the wort in the packet, producing carbon dioxide that will eventually cause the packet to swell up like a balloon. When ready to pitch, cut off one corner of the packet with a pair of sanitized scissors.

Yeast Varieties

This is a list of some of the available varieties of ale and lager yeasts in dry and liquid form. We have included notes on the flavor characteristics and styles suited to each one, as well as a little technical information on their *attenuation* and flocculation rates.

Attenuation refers to the degree of fermentation produced by a yeast. Highly attenuative yeasts tend to produce drier-tasting beers with slightly more alcohol; less attenuative yeasts produce maltier-tasting beers.

Flocculation refers to the tendency of the yeast to form sediment and drop out of solution. Flocculant yeasts tend not to be very attenuative, that is, they tend to stop fermenting and drop out of solution sooner than less-flocculant yeasts. Flocculation is a characteristic that varies depending on conditions in the home brewery, so these guidelines should be considered rough.

Dried Ale Yeast

Edme ale yeast. A fast-acting, highly attenuative yeast with some fruity esters. 11-g (½-ounce) packet.

Glen Brew secret brewer's yeast (ale). Highly attenuative, with a noticeable yeasty flavor. Recommended for brews with a very high specific gravity, i.e., Barleywine ales, old ales. 10-g (½-ounce) packet.

Munton & Fison Muntona ale yeast. Fast-acting, highly

attenuative yeast with some fruity esters. 7-g (¼-ounce) packet.

Nottingham ale yeast. Fast-acting, nutty-tasting yeast with good flocculation. Produces a dry, crisp ale. 5-g ($^1/_5$-ounce) packet.

Red Star ale yeast. Fast-starting, attenuative yeast with unobtrusive taste. 7-g (¼-ounce) packet.

Whitbread ale yeast. Very reliable, fast-starting yeast blend. Has its own unique flavor. The only ale yeast capable of cool-temperature fermentation. 14-g (½-ounce) packet.

Dried Lager Yeast

Yeastlab Amsterdam lager/European lager yeast. This is the same yeast sold in different-size packets. Amsterdam packets are 7 grams (¼ ounce), European packets are 14 grams (½ ounce). A good all-purpose lager yeast that creates a clean, crisp taste. Medium attenuation and flocculation. Produces some sulfury notes early in fermentation.

Liquid Ale Yeast

Wyeast #1214 Belgian ale. Fruity, phenolic, spicy with banana ester. Alcohol tolerant. Highly attenuative and flocculant.

Wyeast #1968 London ale. Bold, woody, slight butterscotch (diacetyl) flavor. Medium attenuation, flocculation. Recommended for most British ales.

Yeastlab A02 American ale. Soft and smooth when fermented cool. Fruity aroma. Medium attenuation, low flocculation.

Yeastlab A05 Irish ale. Mildly acidic with butterscotch (diacetyl) note. Medium attenuation and high flocculation. Recommended for use in stouts and porters.

Yeastlab A07 Canadian ale. Clean and flavorful, fruity when fermented cool. Highly attenuative and flocculant. Recommended for light and cream ales.

Yeastlab A08 Trappist ale. Fruity, phenolic, alcohol tolerant, highly attenuative and flocculant.

Liquid Lager Yeast

Wyeast #2035 American lager. Complex, woody, slightly diacetyl. Medium attenuation and flocculation.

Wyeast #2042 Danish lager. Soft, dry. Recommended for European-style lagers. Medium attenuation, low flocculation.

Wyeast #2112 California lager. Warm-fermenting lager yeast, prefers temperatures around 60°F (16°C). Medium attenuation, high flocculation. Recommended for use in California Common beers.

Yeastlab L31 Pilsner lager. Dry and clean. High attenuation and flocculation. Recommended for German- and Bohemian-style pilsners.

Yeastlab L32 Bavarian lager. Rich, malty, and sweet. Medium attenuation and flocculation. Recommended for bocks, Vienna lagers, Märzens, and Oktoberfests.

Yeastlab L33 Munich lager. Subtle, smooth, and complex. Medium attenuation and flocculation. Some sulfury notes when fresh. Recommended for bocks and European lagers.

Yeastlab L34 St. Louis lager. Clean, crisp, and fruity. High attenuation, medium flocculation. Recommended for American-style pilsners.

Yeastlab L35 California lager. Malty, woody, with some fruitiness. Medium attenuation, high flocculation. Recommended for California Common beers.

Finings

Finings are clarifying aids that are added to the boil or during fermentation. Finings act by precipitating proteins, yeast, and other by-products of brewing out of your beer, resulting in a clearer product.

Irish moss. Sometimes called carrageen, Irish moss is a dried, pulverized seaweed that is added during the boil to help coagulate proteins. It is much more effective if hydrated (soaked) overnight before brewing. Most of our recipes call for 1 teaspoon (5 ml) in 1 cup (240 ml) of warm water. It's a good idea always to add Irish moss to the boil, *whether the recipe calls for it or not.*

Gelatin. Plain, unflavored gelatin is added at bottling time to help settle yeast and proteins during carbonation. It is available at the grocery store. One packet of gelatin added to 1 pint (470 ml) of water is sufficient for 5 gallons (19L) of beer. It is very important not to boil the gelatin — it loses its coagulating power if boiled. Gelatin is easy to use, produces very clear beer, and makes pouring the beer easier (because it coagulates the sediment at the bottom of the bottle). If you must choose only one fining agent, gelatin is your best bet.

English Sugar

Oscar Wilde called the English and Americans two peoples "divided by a common language." This is also true of the instructions provided with kits. Part of the problem, aside from the incompatibility of our measuring systems, lies in the kinds of table sugar we use. In the U.S. we favor refined white sugar, but the British use turbinado or Demerara sugar, very different animals.

Turbinado and Demerara are "raw" (that is, only partly refined) cane sugars. In the brew pot they behave much like brown sugar and contribute some interesting unfermentable characteristics to the beer. Refined white sugar, however, produces only alcohol, thinness, and the cidery flavors of beer made during Prohibition. To brew in the British style, you have to use British sugar.

Brewing with Fruit

Many beginning brewers want to learn how to use fruit in their brewing. This is fairly easy to do if you follow a few basic steps. First, choose a fairly light beer recipe — Leslie's Light Lager or one of the Canadian ales would work well. Light beers allow the most fruit flavor to show through, but some dark beers work well too (i.e., raspberry stout and cherry porter). Then decide if you want to use real fruit.

An easy way for beginners to add fruit flavor to their beers without worrying is to use a fruit concentrate, available at your homebrew store. You can add 2 to 4 ounces (56–110 g) of concentrate with the priming solution at bottling time. Start with a small amount, taste the beer, and add more if necessary.

The process for using real fruit is a little more involved. Roughly 1 to 1½ pounds (½–¾ kg) of fruit per gallon of beer should be enough, but fresh or frozen fruit must be added to hot wort to kill any bacteria or wild yeast that might be on it. Avoid boiling the fruit, however, since this will release pectin (a complex fruit protein) that will make your beer hazy.

First, brew your recipe according to the instructions. Use hop bags to contain any hops added to the boil. Remove the hop bags and shut off the heat. Take your wort's temperature. If you are using frozen fruit, add it if the wort is at least 190°F (88°C) because the fruit will melt and lower the wort temperature quickly. Fresh fruit should be crushed before you add it to the wort, and the wort must be at 160°F (71°C). To prevent the formation of fruit pectin, add pectic enzyme, a wine-making ingredient. About 2½ teaspoons (13 ml) — ½ teaspoon (2 ml) per gallon — will clear up the wort.

Allow the fruited wort to steep for 15–20 minutes. Then pour the whole thing into a 6½-gallon (25L) plastic fermenting bucket. It's not a good idea to use a carboy for this, since fruit particles and matter will block the blowby and cause a wort explosion.

Top up to 5½ gallons (21L) and pitch yeast as usual. (You'll lose some beer when siphoning off the fruit sediment.) Allow the beer and fruit to ferment together for 2 weeks to a month. Then rack the beer to a bottling bucket (a carboy is fine) to complete its fermentation.

When designing recipes for fruit beers, avoid using too many bittering and aroma hops. Their flavors will compete with those of the fruit.

SPENT GRAINS AND SUCH

Homebrewing produces an enormous amount of spent grains, hops, and yeast. Instead of just throwing this stuff out, you should make an effort to compost it. Not everybody can do this, of course, but it's a nice thing to do for the planet. Gardeners can use yeast sediment as slug bait — there's nothing slugs like better, and the little monsters drown in it. Pigs also enjoy the by-products of homebrewing, as we once discovered to our sorrow when a herd of neighboring swine got loose and destroyed our composting bin (and half of our backyard) to get at a carboyful of infected stout.

3

Recipes by Style and Region

THESE BEER RECIPES have been formulated from kits with an emphasis on simplicity, flavor, and a reasonable adherence to style. Some are interpretations of commercially available beers, and some are our own take on traditional favorites. We've included a brief description of each style of beer and some notes on the individual brews to give you an idea of what the final product will be like.

No two brewers ever agree on what constitutes a style. Unless we are entering a contest, we feel how well a beer fits into some rigid and probably arbitrary category is much less important than how enjoyable it is — how its flavor, aroma, body, and color excite the senses and the palate. Of course many brewers find fulfillment in getting their beer styles down to the nth of perfection, and that's fine too. It really all depends on what you like.

The recipes come in two basic types. Those marked by a are for the true beginner. The others are a little more advanced and usually include some grains.

DOUBLE-STAGE FERMENTATION

In Chapter 1 we described single-stage fermentation, where both the primary and secondary fermentations take place in a single plastic container. This method has the advantage of simplicity and is fine for fast-finishing, medium-alcohol brews like bitter. Most ales can be made this way unless they are strongly alcoholic or use a lot of grains, in which case you must use two-stage fermentation. This entails *racking* the beer from the primary fermenter into a secondary fermenter — either the one provided in the equipment set or, better yet, a carboy.

Secondary fermenters are necessary for strong ales and all lagers because they need to age for long periods of time, and it is unwise to leave beer for an extended period on the dregs of the *primary fermentation*. Separate fermentation also results in a clearer beer with less sediment.

Racking the beer just involves siphoning from one container to another, the same process that you use when bottling. It can be done as soon as primary fermentation is complete.

ADDING DRY MALT EXTRACT

The easiest way to add dry malt extract to a recipe using grains is simply to put the extract into your second brew pot and strain the sweet wort from the first brew pot on top of it. Stir to dissolve, then add your extract syrup.

North American Ales

Traditional favorite North American ales include Canadian, Cream, and American.

Canadian Ale

Most Canadian ales are fermented warm and lagered cold. They use 6-row malts and lots of adjuncts for an American-style taste, but they are more generously hopped than lager-ales produced in this country.

 **Maple Leaf Rag Ale**

Initial Gravity: 1.040–1.048   Final Gravity: 1.014–1.016

- 3.3 pounds John Bull Premium Canadian Ale kit (1.5 kg)
- 2 pounds Munton & Fison plain light dry malt extract (.9 kg)
- 1 pound clover honey (.45 kg)
- 1 ounce Cascade hop pellets (28 g)
- 1–2 packets Doric ale yeast
- ¾ cup corn sugar for priming (180 ml)

1. Bring 1½ gallons (6L) of cold water to a boil. Add the extracts and honey and boil for 20 minutes. Add Cascade hops to the last 2 minutes of boil.
2. Strain hot wort into a fermenter containing 1½ gallons (6L) of chilled water. Rinse hops with boiled water. Add enough water to make 5 gallons (19L).
3. Pitch yeast when cool.
4. Ferment at ale temperatures (65° to 70°F, 18° to 21°C).
5. Bottle when fermentation ceases (7–10 days). Age 4 weeks at lager temperatures (40° to 50°F, 4° to 10°C).

BLUENOSE ALE

INITIAL GRAVITY: 1.044–1.052   FINAL GRAVITY: 1.018–1.021

    ½ pound Munton & Fison 60° Lovibond crystal malt (220 g)
    ¾ pound Ireks Munich malt (340 g)
    3.3 pounds John Bull Premium Canadian Ale kit (1.5 kg)
    1 pound Munton & Fison plain light dry malt extract (.45 kg)
    ½ ounce Cascade hop pellets for aroma (14 g)
        Yeastlab A07 Canadian Ale yeast
    ¾ cup corn sugar for priming (180 ml)

1. Add crushed grains to 1½ gallons (6L) of cold water and bring the mixture to a slow boil over 30 minutes. Strain out the grains and rinse with ½ gallon (2L) of boiled water. Add the extracts. Boil for 20 minutes. Add Cascade aroma hops to the final 2 minutes of boil.
2. Strain hot wort into a fermenter containing 1½ gallons (6L) of chilled water. Rinse hops with boiled water. Add enough water to make 5 gallons (19L).
3. Ferment at ale temperatures (65° to 70°F, 18° to 21°C).
4. Bottle when fermentation ceases (1–4 weeks). Age four weeks at lager temperatures (40° to 50°F, 4° to 10°C).

RAINY DAY BLUES BEER

Don Wagoner invented this beer one rainy weekend to keep a friend happy. It worked!

INITIAL GRAVITY: 1.040–1.053   FINAL GRAVITY: 1.012–1.016

    ¼ pound 60° Lovibond crystal malt (110 g)
    ¾ pound Munich malt (340 g)
    4 pounds Mountmellick Export Ale kit (1.8 kg)
    2 pounds Munton & Fison plain light dry malt extract (.9 kg)
        Yeastlab A02 American ale yeast
    ¾ cup corn sugar for priming (180 ml)

1. Put crushed grains in a grain bag and add to 1½ gallons (6L) of cold water. Bring the water to a slow boil over 30 minutes.
2. Strain out the grains and rinse with ½ gallon (2L) of boiled water. Add the extracts and boil for 20 minutes.
3. Pour hot wort into a fermenter containing 1½ gallons (6L) of chilled water. Add enough cold water to make 5 gallons (19L).
4. Pitch yeast when cool.
5. Ferment at ale temperatures (65° to 70°F, 18° to 21°C).
6. Bottle when fermentation ceases (1–3 weeks). Age 3 weeks before drinking.

Cream Ale

Also called blond ale or golden ale, this traditional style, like California Common beer, is a true American product. Unlike California Common, however, cream ale is brewed with top-fermenting ale yeast and cellared at lager temperatures.

 **PROSPERITY CREAM ALE**

INITIAL GRAVITY: 1.035–1.044   FINAL GRAVITY: 1.012–1.016

    4 pounds Ironmaster Imperial Pale Ale kit (1.8 kg)
    2 pounds Dutch extra light dry malt extract (.9 kg)
    ½ ounce Cascade hop pellets for aroma (14 g)
    1–2 packets Munton & Fison ale yeast
    ¾ cup corn sugar for priming (180 ml)

1. Bring 1½ gallons (6L) of cold water to a boil. Add the extracts and boil for 20 minutes. Add Cascade hop pellets to the final 5 minutes of boil.
2. Strain hot wort into a fermenter containing 1½ gallons (6L) of chilled water. Rinse hops with boiled water. Add more water to make up 5 gallons (19L).

3. Pitch yeast when cool.
4. Ferment at ale temperatures (65° to 70°F, 18° to 21°C).
5. Bottle when fermentation is complete (3–10 days). Store at lager temperatures (40° to 50°F, 4° to 10°C) for four weeks.

BEN'S IMPROVED CREAM ALE

This beer is brewed with a larger volume of wort to keep the color light. Accordingly, it's a good idea to use a wort chiller to cool the wort before transferring it to the fermenter. Also, larger volumes of wort are generally harder to control, so you may want to wait until your fourth or fifth batch before tackling this recipe.

INITIAL GRAVITY: 1.040–1.061   FINAL GRAVITY: 1.012–1.017

½ pound Vienna malt (220 g)
4 pounds Premier light hopped syrup (1.8 kg)
3.3 pounds Munton & Fison extra light syrup (1.5 kg)
½ ounce Willamette hop pellets for aroma (14 g)
1–2 packets Munton & Fison ale yeast
¾ cup corn sugar for priming (180 ml)

1. Add Vienna malt to 2½ gallons (6L) of cold water. Bring the water to a slow boil over 30 minutes. When the water boils, strain and rinse the grains with ½ gallon (2L) of boiled water. Add the extracts and bring the mixture to a boil. Boil for 20 minutes, adding hop pellets to the final 5 minutes of boil.
2. Cool the wort with a wort chiller (see Appendix C). Transfer the wort to the fermenter. Add enough cold water to make 5 gallons (19L).
3. Pitch yeast when cool.
4. Ferment at ale temperatures (65° to 70°F, 18° to 21°C).
5. Bottle when fermentation ceases (3–10 days).
6. Lager at cool temperatures (40° to 50°F, 4° to 10°C) for 1 month.

American Pale Ale

American pale ale is nothing like its British cousin. Usually microbrewers call their lightest house ale "pale," to avoid frightening people who usually drink light lager.

 ### SERGEANT PAUL'S HOUSE ALE

This is the only beer Portsmouth's Sergeant Paul will brew, even though his boss, the chief of police, keeps bugging him to try something else. Sergeant Paul knows what he likes. This is a medium-to-light, easy-drinking golden rice ale.

INITIAL GRAVITY: 1.037–1.045   FINAL GRAVITY: 1.006–1.010

  3.3 pounds Premier American Rice Beer kit (1.5 kg)
    2 pounds Munton & Fison plain light dry malt extract (.9 kg)
1–2 packets Doric ale yeast
   ½ ounce Cascade hop plug for dry hopping (14 g)
   ½ ounce East Kent Goldings hop plug for dry hopping (14 g)
   ¾ cup corn sugar for priming (180 ml)

1. Bring 1½ gallons (6L) of cold water to a boil. Add the extracts and boil for 20 minutes.
2. Pour hot wort into a fermenter containing 1½ gallons (6L) of chilled water. Add enough water to make 5 gallons (19L).
3. Pitch yeast when cool.
4. Ferment at ale temperatures (65° to 70°F, 18° to 21°C).
5. When primary fermentation subsides (about 3 days), dry hop with Cascade and East Kent Goldings hop plugs in a hop bag.
6. Bottle when fermentation ceases (5–14 days). Age 3 weeks before drinking.

NORTH AMERICAN LAGERS

Lagers should always be kept at room temperature until the yeast becomes active. This can be anywhere from 12–48 hours depending on temperature, age and type of yeast, and other factors. Don't just stick them in the cold, or they may never ferment.

American Light

American light is a style that needs no introduction, except to say that each new version evolves toward less flavor, less alcohol, and fewer calories than the one before.

If you enjoy the style already, you will like homebrewed varieties even more. This is what to drink when a heavy beer doesn't suit you.

 **GO INTO THE LIGHT LITE LAGER**

Go into the Light uses rice extract to lighten the color and flavor of the brew.

INITIAL GRAVITY: 1.044–1.050   FINAL GRAVITY: 1.009–1.013

> 4 pounds Alexander's hopped malt extract (1.8 kg)
> 3 pounds rice syrup solids (1.4 kg)
> 1–2 packets dry lager yeast
> ¾ cup corn sugar for priming (180 ml)

1. Bring 1½ gallons (6L) of cold water to a boil. Add the extracts and boil for 20 minutes.
2. Pour hot wort into a fermenter containing 1½ gallons (6L) of chilled water. Add more water to make 5 gallons (19L).
3. Pitch yeast when cool.
4. Start at warm temperatures (60° to 70°F, 16° to 21°C), then move to a cool place to ferment at lager temperatures (40° to 50°F, 4° to 10°C).
5. Bottle when fermentation is complete (2–3 weeks). Age cold 4 weeks before drinking.

LESLIE'S LITE LAGER

Leslie's Lite is light in color, unmistakably lagerlike in flavor, and may surprise your nonhomebrewing friends. The use of toasted grains contributes a freshly malty flavor and aroma.

INITIAL GRAVITY: 1.028–1.032   FINAL GRAVITY: 1.010–1.016

- ¼ pound pale malt (110 g)
- 3.3 pounds Black Rock Lager kit (1.5L)
- ½ ounce Cascade hop pellets for bittering (14 g)
- ½ ounce Tettnang hop pellets for aroma (14 g)
  Yeastlab L34 St. Louis lager
- ¾ cup corn sugar for priming (180 ml)

1. Toast the pale malt in a 350°F (178°C) oven for 5–10 minutes, until golden and aromatic. Crush the grains and add them to 1½ gallons (6L) of cold water.
2. Slowly bring the water to a boil over 30 minutes. Strain out the grains and rinse with ½ gallon (2L) of boiled water. Add the malt extract and return to a boil. Add Cascade hop pellets and boil for 45 minutes. Add Tettnang hop pellets to the final 2 minutes of boil.
3. Strain hot wort into a fermenter containing 1½ gallons (6L) of chilled water. Rinse hops with boiled water. Top up with cold water to make 5 gallons (19L).
4. Pitch yeast when cool.
5. Start in a warm place and then move to ferment at lager temperatures (40° to 50°F, 4° to 10°C).
6. Bottle when fermentation is complete (3–6 weeks). Age cold (40° to 50°F, 4° to 10°C) 4 weeks before drinking.

CALIFORNIA COMMON BEER

California Common is one of our native American beers. It was developed on the West Coast before refrigeration, when cold lager temperatures were unattainable and warmth-loving ale yeasts were unavailable. So Californians began to brew a smooth, frothy beverage from lager yeasts at ale temperatures. The product had such an explosive temperament that it was promptly dubbed "steam beer."

Steam Beer is a registered trademark of the Anchor Brewing Company, so the style is now called California Common. It takes a little longer to brew than an ale, but the results are definitely worth it.

Anchor Steam typifies the style, with alelike esters and a thirst-quenching bitter dryness.

 ## Minuteman Common Beer

INITIAL GRAVITY: 1.045–1.051   FINAL GRAVITY: 1.010–1.014

> 4 pounds Munton & Fison Premium malt extract (1.8 kg)
> 2 pounds amber dry malt extract (.9 kg)
> ½ ounce Cascade hop pellets for bittering (14 g)
> ½ ounce Cascade hop pellets for aroma (14 g)
>   Yeastlab L35 California lager
> ¾ cup corn sugar for priming (180 ml)

1. Three days before brewing, activate the yeast pack.
2. Bring 1½ gallons (6L) of cold water to a boil. Add the extracts and ½ ounce (14 g) of Cascade bittering hops. Boil for 60 minutes. Add ½ ounce (14 g) of Cascade aroma hops to the final 5 minutes of boil.
3. Strain hot wort into a fermenter containing 1½ gallons (6L) of chilled water. Rinse hops with boiled water. Add enough water to make 5 gallons (19L).
4. Pitch yeast when cool.
5. Ferment at ale temperatures (65° to 70°F, 18° to 21°C).
6. Bottle when fermentation stops (4–6 weeks). Age at cellar temperature (55°F, 13°C) for 4 weeks.

KRAKATOA COMMON BEER

Our experiments with steamy West Coast beers always seem to involve explosions. Our prize-winning "Turbine" got its name because the airlock blew off and flew high into the air, spinning like a . . . Anyway, take precautions.

INITIAL GRAVITY: 1.034–1.051   FINAL GRAVITY: 1.012–1.018

- ½ pound crystal malt (220 g)
- ½ pound Munich malt (220 g)
- 3.5 pounds Geordie Yorkshire Bitter kit (1.6 kg)
- 2 pounds light dry malt extract (.9 kg)
- 1 ounce Perle hop pellets for bittering (28 g)
- 1 ounce Cascade Pellets for aroma (28 g)
- Wyeast #2112 California lager
- ¾ cup corn sugar for priming (180 ml)

1. Three days before brewing, activate the yeast pack.
2. Add the grains to 1½ gallons (6L) of cold water. Bring the mixture to a slow boil over 30 minutes. Strain out the grains and rinse with ½ gallon (2L) of boiled water. Add extracts and Perle bittering hops. Boil for 60 minutes. Add Cascade aroma hops to the final 3 minutes of boil.
3. Strain hot wort into a fermenter containing 1½ gallons (6L) of chilled water. Rinse hops with boiled water. Top up to 5 gallons (19L).
4. Pitch yeast when cool.
5. Ferment at ale temperatures (65° to 70°F, 18° to 21°C).
6. Bottle when fermentation stops (4–6 weeks) and age at cellar temperature (55°F, 13°C) for 4 weeks.

DRY BEER

Dry beer is, well, dry beer. It's brewed to have few of the characteristics associated with most types of beer, such as a strong aftertaste. It isn't very robust, malty, or hoppy. It's sort of the opposite of the classic microbrew and is, therefore, a good drink for people who aren't crazy about the taste of beer. It's also — or should be — light in alcohol and calories. Dry beer is simple to brew (you don't even need to add hops) and is very refreshing on a hot day. Though it's the ultimate American light, it was actually developed in Japan in the 1980s, but Japanese dry beer, if you ever get a chance to try it, is hoppier than ours.

 ### DRY SALVAGES DRY BEER

INITIAL GRAVITY: 1.026–1.031   FINAL GRAVITY: 1.006–1.009

> 3 pounds Brewmart Dry Beer kit (1.4 kg)
> 1 pound rice syrup solids (.9 kg)
>   Glen Brew secret brewer's yeast
> ¾ cup corn sugar (180 ml) or 1¼ cups dry malt extract for priming (310 ml)

1. Bring 1½ gallons (6L) of cold water to a boil. Add the extracts and boil for 20 minutes.
2. Pour hot wort into a fermenter containing 1½ gallons (6L) of chilled water. Add enough water to make up 5 gallons (19L).
3. Pitch yeast when cool.
4. Ferment at ale temperatures (65° to 70°F, 18° to 21°C).
5. Bottle when fermentation ceases (5–14 days). Age at cellar temperature (55°F, 13°C) 4 weeks before drinking.

"YEAH, BUT IT'S A DRY HEAT" DRY BEER

INITIAL GRAVITY: 1.028–1.034   FINAL GRAVITY: 1.010–1.014

- ½ pound Munich malt (220 g)
- ½ pound pilsner malt (220 g)
- 3 pounds Brewmart Dry Beer kit (1.4 kg)
- 1 pound rice syrup solids (.9 kg)
- 1 teaspoon Irish moss (5 ml)
  Glen Brew secret brewer's yeast or
  Wyeast #2035 American lager
- ¾ cup corn sugar for priming (180 ml)

1. Hydrate the Irish moss in 1 cup (240 ml) of water for 8 hours.
2. Add the malt grains to 1½ gallons (6L) of cold water. Raise the temperature to 150°F (66°C) and steep for 30 minutes.
3. Strain out the grains and rinse with ½ gallon (2L) of boiled water. Add the extracts and the Irish moss and boil for 20 minutes.
4. Pour hot wort into a fermenter containing 1½ gallons (6L) of chilled water. Top up to 5 gallons (19L).
5. Ferment at ale temperatures (65° to 70°F, 18° to 21°C).
6. Bottle when ready (5–10 days), age at cellar temperature (55°F, 13°C) 4 weeks.

RED BEER

For some reason red beer is the craze of the mid-90s. Oregon's Blitz-Weinhard Brewery produces one, and so does Pete's Brewing Company. The big brewers have also entered the market with the likes of Red Dog, Red Wolf, and Elk Mountain Red. But as far as we can see, there's nothing particularly special about red beer — except its color. Otherwise it's a medium-bodied, lightly hopped lager or lager ale.

 ## ROSIE'S RED BEER

Rosie's Red is a light, drinkable, American-style lager. Roasted barley provides the color, dry hopping the flavor.

INITIAL GRAVITY: 1.049–1.058   FINAL GRAVITY: 1.014–1.016

- ⅛ pound roasted barley (57 g)
- 3.3 pounds Premier American Rice Beer kit (1.5 kg)
- 4 pounds Alexander's hopped malt extract (1.8 kg)
- 1–2 packets dried lager yeast
- ½ ounce Cascade hop plug (14 g)
- ¾ cup corn sugar for priming (180 ml)

1. Put crushed grains in a grain bag and place it in 1½ gallons (6L) of cold water. Bring the water to a boil and remove the grain bag. Add the extracts, return the mixture to a boil, and boil for 20 minutes.
2. Pour hot wort into a fermenter containing 1½ gallons (6L) of chilled water. Top up to 5 gallons (19L).
3. Pitch yeast when cool.
4. Primary ferment at room temperature for 3 days. Put Cascade hop plug in a hop bag and place bag in fermenter.
5. Lager at cool temperatures (40° to 50°F, 4° to 10°C).
6. Bottle when fermentation stops (3–6 weeks). Age 4 weeks before drinking.

STOCK LAGER

This isn't exactly a style; it's an interpretation. Sam Adams Stock Lager is a tawny, sweetish lager with a medium body and mild hoppiness.

 ## DUMB COMPASS STOCK LAGER

INITIAL GRAVITY: 1.041–1.046   FINAL GRAVITY: 1.010–1.012

- 3.3 pounds Munton & Fison Premium kit (1.5 kg)
- 2 pounds Munton & Fison amber dry malt extract (.9 kg)
- ½ ounce Hallertau hop pellets for bittering (14 g)
- ½ ounce Tettnang hop pellets for aroma (14 g)
- 1–2 packets dried lager yeast
- ¾ cup corn sugar for priming (180 ml)

1. Bring 1½ gallons (6L) of cold water to a boil. Add the extracts and Hallertau hop pellets and boil for 25 minutes. Add Tettnang hops to the final 5 minutes of boil.
2. Strain hot wort into a fermenter containing 1½ gallons (6L) of chilled water. Rinse hops with boiled water. Add enough cold water to make 5 gallons (19L).
3. Pitch yeast when cool.
4. Start fermentation at room temperatures (60° to 70°F, 16° to 21°C), then move the fermenter to a cool place to allow fermentation to take place at lager temperatures (40° to 50°F, 4° to 10 °C).
5. Bottle when fermentation stops (3–6 weeks). Age 3 weeks before drinking.

BILLY ATTUM'S STOCK LAGER

Don Wagoner has a master's touch when replicating commercial beers. Try this one and see.

INITIAL GRAVITY: 1.044–1.051   FINAL GRAVITY: 1.012–1.016

- ½ pound Cara-Pils malt (220 g)
- ½ pound Munich malt (220 g)
- 3.5 pounds Munton & Fison Premium kit (1.6 kg)
- 2 pounds Munton & Fison amber dry malt extract (.9 kg)
- ½ ounce Hallertau hop pellets for bittering (14 g)
- ½ ounce Tettnang hop pellets for aroma (14 g)
  Wyeast # 2035 American lager
- ¾ cup corn sugar for priming (180 ml)

1. Add grains to 1½ gallons (6L) of cold water and bring the mixture to a slow boil over 30 minutes. Strain out the grains and rinse with ½ gallon (2L) of boiled water. Add extracts and Hallertau hops. Boil for 25 minutes. Add Tettnang hops to the final 2 minutes of boil.
2. Strain hot wort into a fermenter containing 1½ gallons (6L) of chilled water. Rinse hops with boiled water. Add enough cold water to make 5 gallons (19L).
3. Pitch yeast when cool.
4. Start fermentation at room temperatures (60° to 70°F, 16° to 21°C), then move fermenter to a cool place to allow fermentation to continue at lager temperatures (40° to 50°F, 4° to 10°C).
5. Bottle when fermentation ceases (3–6 weeks). Age 3 weeks before drinking.

BELGIAN ALES

Among the numerous Belgian ales are dubbels, duvels, Flanders browns, framboise, krieks, tripels, and whites.

Dubbel

Dubbel is one of the many styles of Belgian Trappist ales produced by monks living in this beer-intensive region. Each monastery has its own style, specialty, and strain of yeast, making it impossible to generalize about them. The monks usually brew an everyday beer, which is not very alcoholic, for their own consumption, and three beers of increasing strength for sale outside the monastery: a single, a double, and a triple. In the case of Chimay, the three beers also have three different characters. Chimay Red is fruity and estery; Chimay White is dry and hoppy; and Chimay Blue is highly complex and so alcoholic that it can be stored like a wine.

English tradition records this verse about the drinking habits of monks:

> *"To drink like a Capuchin is to drink poorly,*
> *To drink like a Benedictine is to drink deeply,*
> *To drink like a Dominican is pot after pot,*
> *But to drink like a Franciscan is to drink the*
>   *cellar dry."*

 **ABBEY ON THE PISCATAQUA**

INITIAL GRAVITY: 1.068–1.070   FINAL GRAVITY: 1.005–1.009

    6.6 pounds Brewferm Tripel kit (2 cans) (3 kg)
      2 teaspoons Fermax yeast nutrient (10 ml)
      1 ounce Styrian Goldings hop plugs for flavoring (28 g)
      1 ounce Saaz hop plugs for aroma (28 g)
      1 packet Whitbread ale yeast
     ¾ cup corn sugar for priming (180 ml)

1. Bring 1½ gallons (6L) of water to a boil. Add the extract and the yeast nutrient and boil for 20 minutes. Add Styrian Goldings flavor hops to the last 10 minutes of boil. Add Saaz aroma hops to the last 2 minutes of boil. Steep for 10 minutes.
2. Strain hot wort into a fermenter containing 1½ gallons (6L) of chilled water. Rinse hops with boiled water. Add enough water to make up 5 gallons (19L).
3. Pitch yeast when cool.
4. Ferment at ale temperatures (65° to 70°F, 18° to 21°C).
5. Bottle when fermentation ceases (7–14 days). Age 6 weeks before drinking.

FRIARY DUBBEL

INITIAL GRAVITY: 1.069–1.072   FINAL GRAVITY: 1.012–1.016

   4 pounds Mahogany Coast Trappist Ale kit (1.8 kg)
   3 pounds amber dry malt extract (1.4 kg)
   ½ pound brown sugar (220 g)
      Yeastlab A08 Trappist ale
   ¾ cup corn sugar for priming (180 ml)

1. Bring 1½ gallons (6L) of cold water to a boil. Add the extracts and brown sugar and boil for 30 minutes.
2. Pour hot wort into a fermenter containing 1½ gallons (6L) of chilled water. Top up to 5 gallons (19L).
3. Pitch yeast when cool.
4. Ferment at ale temperatures (65° to 75°F, 18° to 21°C).
5. Bottle when fermentation ceases (3–6 weeks). Age 6 weeks before drinking.

Duvel

Duvel is a golden Belgian ale that deceives you into thinking it's a harmless pale lager when, in reality, it's a devilishly potent and complex brew. As brewed in Belgium, Duvel derives its demonic nature from a split fermentation process that uses two different yeast strains, followed by two different temperature-controlled lagerings.

 **DON'S DEVIL DUVEL**

Don's Devil is an interesting example of the style. It gets its complexity from the use of honey and liquid Belgian ale yeast.

INITIAL GRAVITY: 1.078–1.080   FINAL GRAVITY: 1.004–1.009

> 6.6 pounds Brewferm Diabolo Belgian Ale kit (2 cans) (3 kg)
> 2 pounds honey (.9 kg)
>   Yeastlab A08 Belgian ale yeast
> ¾ cup corn sugar for priming (180 ml)

1. Before brewing, put the yeast in a warm place and allow it to come to room temperature.
2. Bring 1½ gallons (6L) of cold water to a boil. Add the malt extract and honey and boil for 20 minutes, skimming off the white foam as it appears.
3. Pour hot wort into a fermenter containing 1½ gallons (6L) of chilled water. Add enough cold water to make 5 gallons (19L).
4. Pitch yeast when cool.
5. Ferment at ale temperatures (65° to 70°F, 18° to 21°C).
6. Bottle when fermentation ceases (3–6 weeks). Age 6 weeks before drinking.

Flanders Brown

Flanders Brown is a complex Belgian ale, warm fermented with both wild and tame yeasts. As a result, its flavor is sweet, sour, and unpredictable. Its dark reddish-brown color comes from a long, slow boil. Generally an old batch (2 or more years) and a young batch are bottled together for an even more layered flavor. Ours is only an approximation. Liefman's Brown is a rare, but worthwhile, commercial variety.

PEASANTS' DANCE FLANDERS BROWN

Peasants' Dance uses a slow, large-volume wort boil to achieve the caramelized red color appropriate to the style.

INITIAL GRAVITY: 1.032–1.036   FINAL GRAVITY: 1.015–1.020

> 3.3 pounds Brewferm Old Flemish Brown kit (1.5 kg)
> 2 pounds amber dry malt (.9 kg)
> ⅓ ounce Hallertau hops for aroma (9 g)
> 1 packet Whitbread ale yeast
> ¾ cup corn sugar for priming (180 ml)

1. Bring 2 gallons (7½L) of cold water to a boil. Add the extracts and keep at a slow boil for 2 hours. Add Hallertau hops to the last 5 minutes of boil.
2. Pour hot wort into a fermenter containing 1½ gallons (6L) of cold water. Top up to 5 gallons (19L).
3. Pitch yeast when cool.
4. Ferment at ale temperatures (65° to 70°F, 18° to 21°C).
5. Bottle when fermentation stops (7–10 days). Age 3 weeks before drinking.

GARDEN OF EARTHLY DELIGHTS
FLANDERS BROWN

Garden of Earthly Delights would make a good base for a Belgian framboise with the addition of 6 pounds (2.7 kg) of raspberries (see "Brewing with Fruit" in Chapter 2).

INITIAL GRAVITY: 1.035–1.040   FINAL GRAVITY: 1.019–1.022

- 6 ounces Special B malt (170 g)
- 3.3 pounds Brewferm Old Flemish Brown kit (1.5 kg)
- 2 pounds light dry malt extract (.9 kg)
- ⅓ ounce Saaz hop pellets for aroma (9 g)
- Yeastlab A08 Belgian ale yeast
- ¾ cup corn sugar (180 ml)

1. Put crushed grains in a grain bag and add the bag to 2 gallons (7½L) of cold water. Bring the water to a slow boil over 30 minutes and remove the grain bag. Add the extracts and keep at a slow boil for 2 hours. Add Saaz hops to the final 5 minutes of boil.
2. Strain hot wort into a fermenter containing 1½ gallons (6L) of chilled water. Top up to 5 gallons (19L).
3. Pitch yeast when cool.
4. Ferment at ale temperatures (65° to 70°F, 18° to 21°C).
5. Bottle when fermentation stops (3–6 weeks). Age 3 weeks before drinking.

Framboise

Framboise is usually, but not always, a Belgian lambic ale that has been blended with raspberries to bring on a secondary fermentation. Lambic itself is a strange, soured brew that has been fermented with wild yeast and ancient hops that have been exposed to sunlight to lose their bitterness. Of course, no kit can produce this style without Belgian wild yeasts to ferment it.

Our Framboise de Gambrinus uses honey, extra malt, and authentic Trappist ale yeast to suggest the mysteries of this raspberry oddity. Liefman's Frambozen is an excellent commercial example of the style. It happens not to be a lambic, however; it's a raspberry Flanders Brown. Ours is a basic Belgian fruit ale.

As an interesting variation, both these recipes can be brewed with real raspberries (see "Brewing with Fruit," Chapter 2). Six pounds (2.7 kg) of berries should be enough to brew 5 gallons (19L) of beer.

 **RASPBERRY RIOT FRAMBOISE**

INITIAL GRAVITY: 1.075–1.079   FINAL GRAVITY: 1.007–1.010

- 6.6 pounds Brewferm Framboise kit (2 cans) (3 kg)
- 1 pound Dutch plain extra light dry malt extract (.45 kg)
- 3 teaspoons Fermax yeast nutrient (15 ml)
- 1–2 packets Edme ale yeast
- ¾ cup corn sugar for priming (180 ml)

1. Bring 1½ gallons (6L) of cold water to a boil. Add the extracts and yeast nutrient and boil for 20 minutes.
2. Add hot wort to a fermenter containing 1½ gallons (6L) of chilled water. Add enough water to make 5 gallons (19L).
3. Pitch yeast when cool.
4. Ferment at ale temperatures (65° to 70°F, 18° to 21°C).
5. Bottle when fermentation ceases (7–10 days). Age 3 weeks before drinking.

FRAMBOISE DE GAMBRINUS

Saint Gambrinus is the legendary patron saint of drinkers and brewers. In medieval Austria, a panel with the inscription "Holy Gambrinus, pray for us!" was often erected on the site of a drunkard's fatal accident.

INITIAL GRAVITY: 1.079–1.083   FINAL GRAVITY: 1.008–1.012

- ½ pound 3° Lovibond German crystal malt (220 g)
- ¼ pound Cara-Pils malt (110 g)
- ¼ pound Munich malt (110 g)
- 1 teaspoon Irish moss (5 ml)
- 6.6 pounds Brewferm Framboise kit (2 cans) (3 kg)
- 1 pound clover honey (.45 kg)
- 3 teaspoons Fermax yeast nutrient (15 ml)
- Yeastlab A08 Trappist ale
- ¾ cup corn sugar for priming (180 ml)

1. Three days before brewing, activate the yeast.
2. Hydrate the Irish moss in 1 cup (240 ml) of water for 8 hours.
3. Put crushed malt grains in a grain bag. Add the grain bag to 1½ gallons (6L) of cold water and bring the water to a slow boil over 30 minutes. Strain out the grains and rinse with ½ gallon (2L) of boiled water. Add extracts, Irish moss, yeast nutrient, and honey and boil for 30 minutes.
4. Pour hot wort into a fermenter containing 1½ gallons (6L) of chilled water and add enough water to make 5 gallons (19L).
5. Pitch yeast when cool.
6. Ferment at ale temperatures (65° to 70°F, 18° to 21°C).
7. Bottle when fermentation ceases (3–6 weeks). Age 3 weeks before drinking.

Kriek

Kriek (pronounced "creek") lambic is another entry in the list of unusual Belgian beers. Sour-mashed with plenty of wheat malt and fermented with wild yeast, kriek is so interesting that you might overlook its key ingredient: cherries. In the traditional Belgian kriek cherries are added to the secondary fermentation and allowed to ferment for up to 4 months.

Lindeman's Kriek is a good commercial example of the style. Our recipe is an approximation of a basic Belgian fruit beer, not a lambic.

Like the framboise above, Up the Kriek and Back Porch Kriek can be made with real fruit (see "Brewing with Fruit" in Chapter 2). Five pounds (2.3 kg) of cherries should be enough for 5 gallons (19L) of beer.

 ## UP THE KRIEK

INITIAL GRAVITY: 1.070–1.078   **FINAL GRAVITY: 1.008–1.012**

  6.6 pounds Brewferm Kriek kit (2 cans) (3 kg)
    1 pound light honey (.45 kg)
    3 teaspoons Fermax yeast nutrient (15 ml)
1–2 packets Edme ale yeast
   ¾ cup corn sugar for priming (180 ml)

1. Bring 1½ gallons (6L) of cold water to a boil. Add the extract, honey, and yeast nutrient and boil for 20 minutes.
2. Pour hot wort into a fermenter containing 1½ gallons (6L) of chilled water. Add enough water to make 5 gallons (19L).
3. Pitch yeast when cool.
4. Ferment at ale temperatures (65° to 70°F, 18° to 21°C).
5. Bottle when fermentation ceases (7–10 days). Age 4 weeks before drinking.

BACK PORCH KRIEK

INITIAL GRAVITY: 1.078–1.083   FINAL GRAVITY: 1.009–1.012

- ½ pound Cara-Pils malt (220 g)
- ¼ pound Munich malt (110 g)
- ¼ pound Biscuit malt (110 g)
- 6.6 pounds Brewferm Kriek kit (2 cans) (3 kg)
- 1 pound light honey (.45 kg)
- 3 teaspoons Fermax yeast nutrient (15 ml)
   Yeastlab A08 Trappist ale
- ¾ cup corn sugar for priming (180 ml)

1. Add crushed grains to 1½ gallons (6L) of cold water. Bring the mixture to a slow boil over 30 minutes. Strain out the grains and rinse with ½ gallon (2L) of boiled water. Add the extract, honey, and yeast nutrient and boil for 30 minutes.
2. Pour hot wort into a fermenter containing 1½ gallons (6L) of chilled water. Add enough water to make up 5 gallons (19L).
3. Pitch yeast when cool.
4. Ferment at ale temperatures (65° to 70°F, 18° to 21°C).
5. Bottle when fermentation stops (3–6 weeks). Age 4 weeks before drinking.

Tripel

Tripel is a Trappist brew made by monks using candi sugar, a form of what we know as rock candy. It is fruity, estery, strongly alcoholic, and highly complex. Our version typifies Chimay Tripel. This is enjoyed by the wineglass, not by the pint. It ages well and continues to develop in the bottle, metamorphosing into unlikely and delicious new forms.

 ## BROTHER DENNIS'S TRIPEL X

INITIAL GRAVITY: 1.070–1.079   FINAL GRAVITY: 1.012–1.016

- 6.6 pounds Brewferm Tripel kit (3 kg) (2 cans)
- 2 pounds clover honey (.9 kg)
- 1 pound Dutch extra light malt extract (.45 kg)
- 1½ ounce Styrian Goldings hops for bittering (42 g)
- 1 ounce Styrian Goldings hops for flavoring (28 g)
- ½ ounce Styrian Goldings hops for aroma (14 g)
- Yeastlab A08 Trappist ale yeast
- ¾ cup corn sugar for priming (180 ml)

1. Bring 1½ gallons (6L) of cold water to a boil. Add the extracts and honey. Return the mixture to a boil, add Styrian Goldings bittering hops and boil for 20 minutes. Add Styrian Goldings flavoring hops to the final 10 minutes of boil. Add Styrian Goldings aroma hops to the final 2 minutes of boil. Steep for 5 minutes.
2. Strain hot wort into a fermenter containing 1½ gallons (6L) of chilled water. Top up to 5 gallons (19L).
3. Pitch yeast when cool.
4. Ferment at ale temperatures (65° to 70°F, 18° to 21°C).
5. Bottle when fermentation stops (3–6 weeks). Age 6 weeks before drinking.

CHAT BOTTE TRIPEL

This recipe only looks complicated. You'll need a reserve carboy to age it properly because you won't want to take your regular fermenter out of circulation for two months.

INITIAL GRAVITY: 1.076–1.080   FINAL GRAVITY: 1.016–1.018

1½ pounds Vienna malt (.7 kg)
½ pound Cara-Pils malt (220 g)
¾ pound Ireks Munich malt (340 g)
2 teaspoons gypsum (10 ml)
6.6 pounds Brewferm Tripel kit (2 cans) (3 kg)
3 pounds clover honey (1.4 kg)
1 teaspoon Irish moss (5 ml)
1½ ounce Styrian Goldings hops for bittering (42 g)
1 ounce Styrian Goldings hops for flavoring (28 g)
Wyeast #1214 Belgian ale
1 ounce Styrian Goldings hops for dry hopping (28 g)
¾ cup corn sugar for priming (180 ml)

1. Three days before brewing, activate the yeast.
2. Hydrate the Irish moss in 1 cup (240 ml) of water overnight.
3. Put the crushed grains into a grain bag. Add the grains and gypsum to 1½ gallons (6L) of cold water and bring the mixture to a slow boil over 30 minutes. Strain out the grains and rinse with ½ gallon (2L) of boiled water. Add extracts, honey, and Irish moss and bring the water to a boil. Add Styrian Goldings bittering hops and boil for 25 minutes. Add Styrian Goldings flavoring hops to the last 10 minutes of boil.
4. Strain hot wort into a fermenter containing 1½ gallons (6L) of chilled water. Rinse the hops with boiled water. Add enough cold water to make 5 gallons (19L).
5. Pitch yeast when cool.
6. Ferment at ale temperatures (65° to 70°F, 18° to 21°C). When primary fermentation slows (4–7 days), add Styrian Goldings dry hops (in the hop bag if desired).
7. Bottle when fermentation ceases and yeast has dropped clear (6–8 weeks). Age 12 weeks before drinking.

White Beer

Belgian White is an unusual ale made with wheat malt, honey, orange peel, and coriander seed. It is a dessert ale, with a sweet spiciness and honeylike scent. Belgian White is commercially available in this country as Celis Grand Cru.

 ## LA MALHEUREUSE BELGE GRAND CRU

INITIAL GRAVITY: 1.078–1.086   FINAL GRAVITY: 1.012–1.016

- 6.6 pounds Brewferm Grand Cru kit (2 cans) (3 kg)
- 2 pounds Munton & Fison plain wheat extract (.9 kg)
- 3 teaspoons Fermax yeast nutrient (15 ml)
- 1–2 packets Edme ale yeast
- ¾ cup corn sugar for priming (180 ml)

1. Bring 1½ gallons (6L) of water to a boil. Add the extracts and yeast nutrient and boil for 20 minutes.
2. Pour hot wort into a fermenter containing 1½ gallons (6L) of chilled water. Add enough water to make up 5 gallons (19L).
3. Pitch yeast when cool.
4. Ferment at ale temperatures (65° to 70°F, 18° to 21°C).
5. Bottle when fermentation ceases (7–10 days). Age 3 weeks before drinking.

TEXAN GRAND CRU

After Pieter Celis saved White Beer from extinction in its hometown of Hoegaarden, Belgium, he set up a brewery in Austin, Texas, to brew it. Only in America!

INITIAL GRAVITY: 1.069–1.073   FINAL GRAVITY: 1.009–1.012

- ¼ pound wheat malt (110 g)
- ½ pound Cara-Pils malt (220 g)
- ¼ pound German 3° Lovibond crystal (110 g)
- 6.6 pounds Brewferm Grand Cru kit (2 cans) (3 kg)
- 3 teaspoons Fermax yeast nutrient (15 ml)
- 1 teaspoon Irish moss (5 ml)
  Wyeast #3944 Belgian White Beer
- ¾ cup corn sugar for priming (180 ml)

1. Three days before brewing, activate the yeast pack.
2. Hydrate the Irish moss in 1 cup (240 ml) of water overnight, or up to 8 hours.
3. Add crushed grains to 1½ gallons (6L) of cold water. Bring the mixture to a slow boil over 30 minutes. Strain out the grains and rinse with ½ gallon (2L) of boiled water. Add the extracts, yeast nutrient and Irish moss, and and boil for 20 minutes.
4. Pour hot wort into a fermenter containing 1½ gallons (6L) of chilled water.
5. Pitch yeast when cool.
6. Ferment at standard ale temperatures (65° to 70°F, 18° to 21°C).
7. Bottle when fermentation ceases (3–6 weeks). Age 3 weeks before drinking.

BRITISH ALES

British ales include bitters and ESB ("extra-special bitters"), brown ales, India pale ales, mild ales, old ales, pale ales, porters, stouts, strong ales, and Yorkshire bitters.

Bitter

Bitter is the national drink of Great Britain. It comes in a seemingly endless number of local varieties, all brewed to different strengths, colors, and proportions of bitterness to sweetness. In general, bitter is cask-carbonated, dry, mildly hopped, and brewed from low gravities (and is therefore light in alcohol). This is because pub crawlers in Britain drink to be sociable, not to get drunk.

 **MOME RATHS BITTER**

INITIAL GRAVITY: 1.033–1.039   FINAL GRAVITY: 1.014–1.016

   3.5 pounds Cooper's Bitter kit (1.6 kg)
   1½ pounds Munton & Fison plain amber dry malt extract (.7 kg)
   ½ ounce East Kent Goldings hop plug for aroma (14 g)
   1–2 packets Nottingham ale yeast
   ½ cup corn sugar (125 ml) or ¾ cup dry malt extract for priming (180 ml)

1. Bring 1½ gallons (6L) of cold water to a boil. Add the extracts and boil for 20 minutes. Add East Kent Goldings aroma hops to the last 5 minutes of boil.
2. Strain hot wort into a fermenter containing 1½ gallons (6L) of chilled water. Rinse hops with boiled water. Add enough water to make 5 gallons (19L).
3. Pitch yeast when cool.
4. Ferment at ale temperatures (65° to 70°F, 18° to 21°C).
5. Bottle when fermentation ceases (7–10 days). Age 2 weeks.

TRAFALGAR BITTER

INITIAL GRAVITY: 1.037–1.045 FINAL GRAVITY: 1.012–1.016

- ½ pound 40° Lovibond crystal malt (220 g)
- 1 teaspoon gypsum (5 ml)
- 4 pounds Telford's Premium Bitter kit (1.8 kg)
- 1½ pounds plain light dry malt extract (.7 kg)
- ½ ounce Fuggles hop plug for bittering (14 g)
- ½ ounce East Kent Goldings hop plug for aroma (14 g)
- 1–2 packets Nottingham ale yeast
- ½ cup corn sugar for priming (125 ml)

1. Add the gypsum and crystal malt to 1½ gallons (6L) of cold water. Bring the mixture to a slow boil over 30 minutes. Strain out the grains and rinse with ½ gallon (2L) of boiled water. Add the extracts and Fuggles bittering hops and boil for 60 minutes. Add East Kent Goldings aroma hops to the final 5 minutes of boil.
2. Strain hot wort into a fermenter containing 1½ gallons (6L) of chilled water. Rinse hops with boiled water.
3. Pitch yeast when cool.
4. Ferment at ale temperatures (65° to 70°F, 18° to 21°C).
5. Bottle when fermentation ceases (7–10 days). Age 2–3 weeks before drinking.

Extra-Special Bitter

Extra-special bitter, or ESB, is brewed at a slightly higher specific gravity and with a bit more hoppiness than your average, or "ordinary," bitter. There is also a "special" bitter with values that fall between the two. Bitter is such a huge and diverse style that it's almost impossible to quantify; one person's ESB is another's victory ale, or whatever. This frothy-headed brew only recently became popular stateside.

 **VICTORIA REGINA ESB**

INITIAL GRAVITY: 1.036–1.044   FINAL GRAVITY: 1.014–1.018

> 3 pounds Brewmart Strong Export Bitter kit (1.4 kg)
> 2 pounds plain amber dry malt extract (.9 kg)
> ¼ cup brown sugar (packed) (60 ml)
> ½ ounce Fuggles hop plug for aroma (14 g)
> 1 packet Whitbread ale yeast
> ½ cup corn sugar for priming (125 ml)

1. Bring 1½ gallons (6L) of cold water to a boil. Add the extracts and brown sugar and boil for 20 minutes. Add Fuggles hop plug to the final 5 minutes of boil.
2. Strain hot wort into a fermenter containing 1½ gallons (6L) of chilled water. Rinse hops with boiled water. Add enough water to make up 5 gallons (19L).
3. Pitch yeast when cool.
4. Ferment at ale temperatures (65° to 70°F, 18° to 21°C).
5. Bottle when fermentation stops (7–10 days). Age 2–3 weeks.

BOBBIE'S WHITECHAPEL ESB

INITIAL GRAVITY: 1.040–1.054   FINAL GRAVITY: 1.014–1.019

- ¾ pound 60° Lovibond crystal malt (340 g)
- 2 teaspoons gypsum (10 ml)
- 4 pounds John Bull Premium Traditional Bitter kit (1.8 kg)
- 2 pounds plain light dry malt extract (.9 kg)
- 1 ounce Chinook hop pellets for bittering (28 g)
- ½ ounce Willamette hop plug for aroma (14 g)
- ½ ounce East Kent Goldings hop plug for aroma (14 g)
- 1 packet Whitbread ale yeast
- ½ cup corn sugar for priming (125 ml)

1. Add the gypsum and crushed crystal malt grains to 1½ gallons (6L) of cold water. Bring the mixture to a slow boil over 30 minutes. Strain out the grains and rinse with ½ gallon (2L) of boiled water. Add the extracts and Chinook hop pellets and boil for 45 minutes. Add Willamette hop plug and boil for 10 minutes. Add East Kent Goldings hop plug to the last 5 minutes of boil.
2. Strain hot wort into a fermenter containing 1½ gallons (6L) of chilled water. Rinse hops with boiled water. Add enough water to make up 5 gallons (19L).
3. Pitch yeast when cool.
4. Ferment at ale temperatures (65° to 70°F, 18° to 21°C).
5. Bottle when fermentation ceases (7–10 days). Age 2–3 weeks.

Brown Ale

Brown ale, as typified by Newcastle Brown (from that northeastern English industrial city), is a mild, nutty, lightly hopped, and fairly low-alcohol beer. There is also a less well-known, darker, maltier version brewed in the south of England. This sweet, chewy beer, almost suited to dessert, is emulated in the U.S. by Brooklyn Brown Dark Ale.

 **BABY BEAR BROWN ALE**

Baby Bear Brown Ale is of the southern school: malty, sweet, and full-bodied, but with greater strength than most brown ales.

INITIAL GRAVITY: 1.065–1.071   FINAL GRAVITY: 1.016–1.019

- 4 pounds Ironmaster Northern Brown Ale kit (1.8 kg)
- 3.75 pounds Cooper's Australian Draught kit (1.7 kg)
- ½ teaspoon Irish moss (2 ml)
- 2 packets Munton & Fison ale yeast
- ½ cup corn sugar for priming (125 ml)

1. Hydrate the Irish moss overnight in 1 cup (240 ml) of water.
2. Bring 1½ gallons (6L) of cold water to a boil. Add the extracts and Irish moss and boil for 20 minutes.
3. Pour hot wort into a fermenter containing 1½ gallons (6L) of chilled water. Top up to make 5 gallons (19L).
4. Pitch yeast when cool.
5. Ferment at ale temperatures (65° to 70°F, 18° to 21°C).
6. Bottle when fermentation stops (7–10 days). Age 2 weeks.

Big D's Best Brown Ale

INITIAL GRAVITY: 1.039–1.057　　　　　FINAL GRAVITY: 1.015–1.019

½ pound chocolate malt (220 g)
1 pound 60° Lovibond Munton & Fison crystal malt (.45 kg)
4 pounds Mountmellick Brown Ale kit (1.8 kg)
2 pounds Munton & Fison plain light dry malt extract (.9 kg)
1 teaspoon Irish moss (5 ml)
½ ounce Fuggles hops for flavoring (14 g)
½ ounce Fuggles hops for aroma (14 g)
1 packet Whitbread ale yeast
1 ounce East Kent Goldings dry hops (28 g)
½ cup corn sugar for priming (125 ml)

1. Hydrate the Irish moss in 1 cup (240 ml) of water overnight, or up to 8 hours.
2. Put the crushed grains in a grain bag and add to 1½ gallons (6L) of cold water. Bring the mixture to a slow boil over 30 minutes. Strain out the grains and rinse with ½ gallon (2L) of boiled water. Add the extracts and Irish moss and boil for 30 minutes. Add ½ ounce (14 g) Fuggles hops to the final 5 minutes of boil. Add ½ ounce (14 g) Fuggles aroma hops to the final 2 minutes of boil.
3. Strain hot wort into a fermenter containing 1½ gallons (6L) of chilled water. Rinse hops with boiled water. Add enough cold water to make up 5 gallons (19L).
4. Pitch yeast when cool.
5. Ferment at ale temperatures (65° to 70°F, 18° to 21°C). When primary fermentation subsides (about 3 days), add East Kent Goldings dry hops to the fermenter.
6. Bottle when fermentation ceases (7–10 days). Age 3 weeks before drinking.

India Pale Ale

India Pale Ale (IPA) dates from the height of the British Raj. It is a hoppy, malty, stronger version of pale ale that was originally designed to weather the trip from breweries in London to thirsty British officers stationed in Bombay and the Punjab.

 **GATEWAY TO INDIA IPA**

INITIAL GRAVITY: 1.060–1.072   FINAL GRAVITY: 1.014–1.019

- 6.6 pounds Black Rock East India Pale Ale kit (3 kg)
- 2.2 pounds Premier hopped malt extract (1 kg)
- ½ ounce East Kent Goldings hop plug for aroma (14 g)
- ½ ounce East Kent Goldings hop plug for dry hopping (14 g)
- 1 packet Whitbread ale yeast
- ⅔ cup corn sugar for priming (160 ml)

1. Bring 1½ gallons (6L) of water to a boil. Add the extracts, return the mixture to a boil, and boil for 20 minutes. Add East Kent Goldings flavoring hops to the final 5 minutes of boil. Steep for 5 minutes.
2. Strain hot wort into a fermenter containing 1½ gallons (6L) of chilled water. Top up to 5 gallons (19L).
3. Pitch yeast when cool.
4. Ferment at ale temperatures (65° to 70°F, 18° to 21°C). When fermentation slows, add East Kent Goldings dry hops in a hop bag.
5. Bottle when fermentation stops (1–2 weeks). Age 3 weeks before drinking.

GANESHA'S RAT IPA

INITIAL GRAVITY: 1.044–1.055   FINAL GRAVITY: 1.014–1.018

- ½ pound toasted pale malt (220 g)
- ¼ pound 60° Lovibond British crystal malt (110 g)
- 4 pounds Ironmaster Pale Ale kit (1.8 kg)
- 2¼ pounds Munton & Fison amber dry malt extract (1 kg)
- 1 ounce Fuggles hop pellets for bittering (28 g)
- ½ ounce East Kent Goldings hop plug for aroma (14 g)
- 1 packet Whitbread ale yeast
- ½ ounce East Kent Goldings hop plug for dry hopping (14 g)
- ⅔ cup corn sugar for priming (160 ml)

1. Toast pale malt in a 350°F (178°C) oven for 10 minutes. Allow the malt to cool, then crush it.
2. Crush all the malts and add to 1½ gallons (6L) of cold water. Bring the mixture to a boil over 30 minutes. Strain out the grains and rinse with ½ gallon (2L) of boiled water. Add the extracts and return the mixture to a boil. Add Fuggles hop pellets and boil for 30 minutes. Add ½ ounce (14 g) East Kent Goldings aroma hops to the final 5 minutes of boil. Steep for 5 minutes.
3. Strain hot wort into a fermenter containing 1½ gallons (6L) of chilled water. Top up to 5 gallons (19L).
4. Pitch yeast when cool.
5. Ferment at ale temperatures (65° to 70°F, 18° to 21°C). When fermentation slows, add ½ ounce (14 g) East Kent Goldings dry hops in a hop bag.
6. Bottle when fermentation stops (1–2 weeks). Age 2 weeks before drinking.

Mild

In the old days, a British pub would have two kinds of beer: mild and bitter. Since the recipes varied from pub to pub, mild ales could be quite hoppy and alcoholic, provided they were less hoppy than the house bitter.

Today mild has become a rarer and more straightforward style than bitter. It's dark-colored, lightly hopped, and mildly alcoholic, making it a good thirst-quencher at the end of a hard day's work.

 DISGUISED AS A MILD-MANNERED MILD

INITIAL GRAVITY: 1.033–1.044   FINAL GRAVITY: 1.010–1.014

- 3.5 pounds Geordie Mild kit (1.6 kg)
- 2 pounds dark dry malt extract (.9 kg)
- ½ teaspoon Irish moss (2 ml)
- 2 ounces Cascade hops for aroma (56 g)
- 1 packet Edme ale yeast
- ⅔ cup corn sugar (160 ml) or 1 cup dry malt extract for priming (250 ml)

1. Hydrate the Irish moss in 1 cup (240 ml) of water overnight, or up to 8 hours.
2. Bring 1½ gallons (6L) of water to a boil. Add the malt extracts and boil for 20 minutes. Add Cascade aroma hops to the last 2 minutes of boil.
3. Strain hot wort into a fermenter containing 1½ gallons (6L) chilled water. Rinse hops with boiled water. Add enough water to make 5 gallons (19L).
4. Pitch yeast when cool.
5. Ferment at ale temperatures (65° to 70°F, 18° to 21°C).
6. Bottle when fermentation ceases (7–10 days). Age 2 weeks.

CRYSTAL PALACE MILD

INITIAL GRAVITY: 1.040–1.050   FINAL GRAVITY: 1.014–1.018

- ¼ pound Cara-Pils malt (110 g)
- ½ pound 40° Lovibond crystal malt (220 g)
- ½ pound Munich malt (220 g)
- 4 pounds Telford's Mild Ale kit (1.8 kg)
- 2 pounds Munton & Fison plain light dry malt extract (.9 kg)
- 1 ounce Fuggles hop pellets for bittering (28 g)
- ½ ounce East Kent Goldings hop plug for aroma (14 g)
  Wyeast #1968 London Ale
- ¾ cup corn sugar for priming (180 ml)

1. Three days before brewing, activate the yeast pack.
2. Add crushed grains to 1½ gallons (6L) of cold water and bring the mixture to a slow boil. Strain out the grains and rinse with ½ gallon (2L) of boiled water. Add the extracts and Fuggles bittering hops and boil for 60 minutes. Add East Kent Goldings hop plug to the final 3 minutes of boil.
3. Strain hot wort into a fermenter containing 1½ gallons (6L) of chilled water. Rinse hops with boiled water. Add enough cold water to make 5 gallons (19L).
4. Pitch yeast when cool.
5. Ferment at ale temperatures (65° to 70°F, 18° to 21°C).
6. Bottle when fermentation ceases (2–3 weeks). Age 3 weeks before drinking.

Old Ale

This is a rich, medium dark ale, often on draft, thoroughly aged, and a strength second only to barley wine. Examples are Old Thumper and Old Peculier. Traditionally, half a pint of old and half a pint of bitter are called a "mother-in-law."

 **OLD BALDY**

A simple and powerful brew. The molasses adds richness and buttery undertones.

INITIAL GRAVITY: 1.065–1.068   FINAL GRAVITY: 1.014–1.018

   6.6 pounds Munton & Fison Old Ale kit (2 cans) (3 kg)
     1 pound light dry malt extract (.45 kg)
    ½ cup unsulfured molasses (125 ml)
     1 packet Whitbread ale yeast
    ½ cup corn sugar for priming (125 ml)

1. Bring 1½ gallons (6L) of cold water to a boil. Add the extracts and molasses and boil for 30 minutes.
2. Pour hot wort into a fermenter containing 1½ gallons (6L) of chilled water. Top up to 5 gallons (19L).
3. Pitch yeast when cool.
4. Ferment at ale temperatures (65° to 70°F, 18° to 21°C).
5. Bottle when fermentation stops (1–3 weeks). Age 3 weeks before drinking.

OLD CONTEMPTIBLE

INITIAL GRAVITY: 1.070–1.072   FINAL GRAVITY: 1.014–1.019

- ¾ pound 60° Lovibond crystal malt (340 g)
- ¼ pound mild ale malt (110 g)
- 3.3 pounds Munton & Fison Old Ale kit (1.5 kg)
- 4 pounds light dry malt extract (1.8 kg)
- ½ cup unsulfured molasses (125 ml)
- 1 ounce Brewer's Gold hop pellets for bittering (28 g)
- ½ ounce East Kent Goldings hop pellets for aroma (14 g)
- 1 packet Whitbread ale yeast
- ½ cup corn sugar for priming (125 ml)

1. Put the grains in a grain bag and add to 1½ gallons (6L) of cold water. Bring the water to a slow boil over 30 minutes. Strain out the grains and rinse with ½ gallon (2L) of boiled water. Add the extracts and molasses and return the mixture to a boil. Add Brewer's Gold hop pellets and boil for 60 minutes. Add East Kent Goldings hop pellets to the last 3 minutes of boil. Steep for 5 minutes.
2. Strain hot wort into a fermenter containing 1½ gallons (6L) of chilled water. Top up to 5 gallons (19L).
3. Pitch yeast when cool.
4. Ferment at ale temperatures (65° to 70°F, 18° to 21°C).
5. Bottle when fermentation stops (1–3 weeks). Age 3 weeks before drinking.

Pale Ale

Pale ale is an amber-to-copper-colored, bitter, malty beer of medium body and alcoholic strength. It is called "pale" only because it was lighter in color than the porters and stouts that were popular at the time of its invention. Pale ale may be called the big brother of bitter. It is well represented in the U.S. by Pike Place Pale Ale.

 **BRASS NOSE PALE ALE**

INITIAL GRAVITY: 1.044–1.055 FINAL GRAVITY: 1.014–1.018

  3.3 pounds Black Rock East India Pale Ale kit (1.5 kg)
  3.3 pounds Brewmaker IPA kit (1.5 kg)
   ½ ounce East Kent Goldings hop plug for aroma (14 g)
   1 packet Whitbread ale yeast
   ½ ounce East Kent Goldings hop plug for flavoring (14 g)
   ⅔ cup corn sugar for priming (160 ml)

1. Bring 1½ gallons (6L) of water to a boil. Add the extracts, return the mixture to a boil, and boil for 20 minutes. Add ½ ounce (14 g) East Kent Goldings flavoring hops to the final 5 minutes of boil. Steep for 5 minutes.
2. Strain hot wort into a fermenter containing 1½ gallons (6L) of chilled water. Top up to 5 gallons (19L).
3. Pitch yeast when cool.
4. Ferment at ale temperatures (65° to 70°F, 18° to 21°C). When fermentation slows, add ½ ounce (14 g) East Kent Goldings dry hops in a hop bag.
5. Bottle when fermentation stops (1–2 weeks). Age 2 weeks before drinking.

MANCHESTER COLLEGE PALE ALE

INITIAL GRAVITY: 1.044–1.055   FINAL GRAVITY: 1.014–1.018

- ½ pound toasted pale malt (220 g)
- 3.3 pounds Brewmaker IPA kit (1.5 kg)
- 2 pounds Munton & Fison amber dry malt extract (.9 kg)
- ½ ounce East Kent Goldings hop plug for aroma (14 g)
- 1 packet Whitbread ale yeast
- ⅔ cup corn sugar for priming (160 ml)

1. Toast pale malt in a 350°F (178°C) oven for 10 minutes. Allow the malt to cool, then crush it.
2. Add the crushed malt to 1½ gallons (6L) of cold water, and bring the mixture to a boil over 30 minutes. Strain out the grains and rinse with ½ gallon (2L) of boiled water. Add extracts and return to a boil for 20 minutes. Add East Kent Goldings aroma hops to the final 5 minutes of boil. Steep for 5 minutes.
3. Strain hot wort into a fermenter containing 1½ gallons (6L) of chilled water. Top up to 5 gallons (19L).
4. Pitch yeast when cool.
5. Ferment at ale temperatures (65° to 70°F, 18° to 21°C).
6. Bottle when fermentation stops (1–2 weeks). Age 2 weeks before drinking.

Porter

Porter is a medium-bodied, moderately hopped dark ale of medium alcoholic strength. Once on the verge of extinction, the tasty brew has made a dramatic comeback both in the homebrew and microbrew worlds. Porter was the workingman's beer of the eighteenth and nineteenth centuries and a favorite of George Washington. A hearty concoction traditionally filled with odd ingredients such as chocolate and licorice, it was first enjoyed by London's porters — thus its name.

 **ADMIRABLE PORTER**

INITIAL GRAVITY: 1.045–1.056   FINAL GRAVITY: 1.014–1.019

    4 pounds Mahogany Coast London Porter kit (1.8 kg)
    3 pounds Northwest Gold Extract Syrup (1.4 kg)
    ½ ounce Kent Goldings hops for bittering (14 g)
    ½ ounce Kent Goldings hops for aroma (14 g)
    1 packet Whitbread Ale yeast
    ½ cup corn sugar for priming (125 ml)

1. Bring 1½ gallons (6L) of cold water to a boil. Add the extracts and ½ ounce (14 g) Kent Goldings bittering hops and boil for 60 minutes. Add finishing hops to the final 2 minutes of boil.
2. Strain hot wort into a fermenter containing 1½ gallons (6L) of chilled water. Rinse hops with boiled water. Add enough water to make 5 gallons (19L).
3. Pitch yeast when cool.
4. Ferment at ale temperatures (65° to 70°F, 18° to 21°C).
5. Bottle when fermentation stops (1–2 weeks). Age 2 weeks.

DIRTY BILL PORTER

INITIAL GRAVITY: 1.048–1.063   FINAL GRAVITY: 1.012–1.018

- ½ pound crystal malt (220 g)
- ½ pound chocolate malt (220 g)
- ¼ pound black malt (110 g)
- 4 pounds Mahogany Coast London Porter Kit (1.8 kg)
- 3 pounds plain amber dry malt extract (1.4 kg)
- 1 ounce Northern Brewer hop plug for bittering (28 g)
- 1 teaspoon Irish moss (5 ml)
- ½ ounce Styrian Goldings hop plug for aroma (14 g)
- 1 packet Whitbread ale yeast
- ⅔ cup corn sugar for priming (160 ml)

1. Hydrate the Irish moss in 1 cup (240 ml) of water for 8 hours.
2. Add the malt grains to 1½ gallons (6L) of cold water. Bring the mixture to a slow boil over 30 minutes. Strain out the grains and rinse with ½ gallon (2L) of boiled water. Add the extracts, Northern Brewer bittering hops, and the Irish moss and boil for 60 minutes. Add Styrian Goldings aroma hops to the final 5 minutes of boil.
3. Strain hot wort into a fermenter containing 1½ gallons (6L) of chilled water. Rinse hops with boiled water. Add enough cold water to make 5 gallons (19L).
4. Pitch yeast when cool.
5. Ferment at ale temperatures (65° to 70°F, 18° to 21°C).
6. Bottle when fermentation stops (1–2 weeks). Age 2 weeks.

Stout

The national beer of Ireland, stout was originally a strong style of porter called "stout-porter." It is a black, bitter, and complex brew, deriving much of its character from roasted barley. Dry stouts include the famous Guinness, which was for many of us our first taste of an imported beer, and the lesser-known (in this country) Murphy's and Beamish. They are usually fairly low in alcohol, with no hop flavor or aroma but plenty of bitterness.

Sweet, English, or milk stouts are less bitter and more alcoholic than dry stouts, and they achieve their sweet character through the addition of unfermentable lactose (milk sugar). Commercial examples of the style include Mackeson Stout and Tooth's Sheaf Stout.

 ## "BIT O' THE CREATURE" IRISH DRY STOUT

INITIAL GRAVITY: 1.040–1.051   FINAL GRAVITY: 1.010–1.014

- 4 pounds Mountmellick Famous Irish Stout kit (1.8 kg)
- 2 pounds Munton & Fison plain dark dry malt extract (.9 kg)
- 1 ounce Bullion leaf hops for bittering (28 g)
- 1–2 packets Cordon Brew Stout yeast
- ⅔ cup corn sugar (160 ml) or 1 cup dry malt extract for priming (240 ml)

1. Bring 1½ gallons (6L) of cold water to a boil. Add the extracts and Bullion bittering hops and boil for 60 minutes.
2. Strain into a fermenter with 1½ gallons (6L) of chilled water. Rinse hops with boiled water. Add enough water to make 5 gallons (19L).
3. Pitch yeast when cool.
4. Ferment at standard ale temperatures (65° to 70°F, 18° to 21°C).
5. Bottle when fermentation ceases (2–3 weeks). Age 3–4 weeks.

BILLY ATTUM'S CREAM STOUT

This brew straddles the styles of dry and milk stouts. It's black, has a nice head, and is smooth with just a trace of hops.

INITIAL GRAVITY: 1.062–1.079   FINAL GRAVITY: 1.016–1.018

- ½ pound 60° Lovibond crystal malt (220 g)
- ½ pound chocolate malt (220 g)
- ½ pound Cara-Pils malt (220 g)
- ¼ pound roasted barley (110 g)
- 6.6 pounds Edme Stout kit (3 kg)
- 1 pound Morgan's crystal malt extract (.45 kg)
- 1 teaspoon Irish moss (5 ml)
- 1 ounce Fuggles hops for bittering (28 g)
- ½ ounce Cascade hop plug for aroma (14 g)
- Yeastlab A05 Irish ale yeast
- ½ cup corn sugar for priming (125 ml)

1. Hydrate the Irish moss overnight, or up to 8 hours.
2. Put the crushed grains in a grain bag and add to 1½ gallons (6L) of cold water. Bring the mixture to a slow boil over 30 minutes. Strain out the grains and rinse with ½ gallon (2L) of boiled water. Add the extracts, Irish moss, and Fuggles bittering hops and boil for 60 minutes. Add Cascade hop plug to the last 3 minutes of boil.
3. Strain hot wort into a fermenter containing 1½ gallons (6L) of chilled water. Rinse hops with boiled water. Add enough cold water to make 5 gallons (19L).
4. Pitch yeast when cool.
5. Ferment at ale temperatures (65° to 70°F, 18° to 21°C).
6. Bottle when fermentation ceases (2–4 weeks). Age 4 weeks before drinking.

Strong Ale

Strong ale is one of a family of ales brewed in Scotland that includes light ales, export ales, and "wee heavies." Strong ale is a malty, tawny-colored, strongly alcoholic, and estery ale with moderate bitterness for its sweetness.

HERCULES STRONG ALE

INITIAL GRAVITY: 1.061–1.050   FINAL GRAVITY: 1.016–1.020

- 4 pounds Laaglander Strong Ale kit (1.8 kg)
- 3 pounds Munton & Fison plain light dry malt extract (1.4 kg)
- 1½ ounce Fuggles hop pellets for bittering (42 g)
- ½ ounce Willamette hop pellets for aroma (14 g)
- ½ ounce East Kent Goldings hop plug for aroma (14 g)
- 1–2 packets Edme ale yeast
- ¾ cup corn sugar for priming (180 ml)

1. Bring 1½ gallons (6L) of cold water to a boil. Add the extracts and Fuggles bittering hops and boil for 60 minutes. Add Willamette hop pellets to the final 5 minutes of boil. Add East Kent Goldings hop plug to the final 2 minutes of boil.
2. Strain hot wort into a fermenter containing 1½ gallons (6L) of chilled water. Rinse hops with boiled water. Add enough water to make 5 gallons (19L).
3. Pitch yeast when cool.
4. Ferment at ale temperatures (65° to 70°F, 18° to 21°C).
5. Bottle when fermentation ceases (10–14 days). Age 4 weeks before drinking.

SAMSON STRONG ALE

INITIAL GRAVITY: 1.053–1.069   FINAL GRAVITY: 1.014–1.020

- ¾ pound 60° Lovibond Munton & Fison crystal malt (350 g)
- ¼ pound Cara-Pils malt (110 g)
- 4 pounds Laaglander Strong Ale kit (1.8 kg)
- 3 pounds Munton & Fison plain light dry malt extract (1.4 kg)
- 1½ ounce Fuggles hop pellets for bittering (42 g)
- ½ ounce Willamette hop pellets for aroma (14 g)
- ½ ounce East Kent Goldings hop plug for aroma (14 g)
  Wyeast #1728 Scottish Ale
- ¾ cup corn sugar for priming (180 ml)

1. Add crushed grains to 1½ gallons (6L) of cold water and bring the mixture to a slow boil over 30 minutes. Strain out the grains and rinse with ½ gallon (2L) of boiled water. Add the extracts and Fuggles bittering hops and boil for 60 minutes. Add Willamette flavoring hops to the last 5 minutes of boil. Add East Kent Goldings aroma hops to the final 2 minutes of boil.
2. Strain hot wort into a fermenter containing 1½ gallons (6L) of chilled water. Rinse hops with boiled water. Add enough water to make 5 gallons (19L).
3. Pitch yeast when cool.
4. Ferment at ale temperatures (65° to 70°F, 18° to 21°C).
5. Bottle when fermentation ceases (2–3 weeks). Age 4 weeks before drinking.

Yorkshire Bitter

The bitters brewed in this area of England are so different as to constitute a style all by themselves. These are maltier and more complex than their southern cousins. Yorkshire bitters have flavors ranging from butterscotch to banana. Traditionally they are fermented in shallow, open stone vessels known as Yorkshire Squares.

 ## GRAND OLD DUKE'S YORKSHIRE BITTER

INITIAL GRAVITY: 1.040–1.046   FINAL GRAVITY: 1.014–1.019

- 3.5 pounds Geordie Yorkshire Bitter kit (1.6 kg)
- 2 pounds Munton & Fison extra light dry malt extract (.9 kg)
- ⅔ cup molasses (160 ml)
- 1–2 packets Edme ale yeast
- ⅔ cup corn sugar for priming (160 ml)

1. Bring 1½ gallons (6L) of cold water to a boil. Add the extracts and molasses and boil for 20 minutes.
2. Pour hot wort into a fermenter containing 1½ gallons (6L) of chilled water. Top up to 5 gallons (19L).
3. Pitch yeast when cool.
4. Ferment at ale temperatures (65° to 70°F, 18° to 21°C).
5. Bottle when fermentation ceases (7–10 days). Age 3 weeks before drinking.

BILLARD'S YORKSHIRE BITTER

Billard's Yorkshire uses a large, slow wort boil to achieve the caramelization appropriate to the style. Brown sugar and specialty malts contribute interesting side flavors.

INITIAL GRAVITY: 1.049–1.055   FINAL GRAVITY: 1.018–1.020

    4 ounces Special B malt (110 g)
    2 ounces chocolate malt (57 g)
    2 ounces 90° Lovibond British crystal malt (57 g)
    4 pounds Munton & Fison Yorkshire Bitter kit (1.8 kg)
    2 pounds Munton & Fison extra light dry malt extract (1.8 kg)
    ½ pound dark brown sugar or Demerara sugar (220 g)
      Wyeast #1728 Scottish ale
    ⅔ cup corn sugar for priming (160 ml)

1. Put crushed grains in a grain bag and add the bag to 2 gallons (8L) of cold water. Bring the mixture to a slow boil over 30 minutes. Strain out the grains and rinse with ½ gallon (2L) of boiled water. Add the extracts and brown sugar and keep the mixture at a slow boil for 2 hours.
2. Pour the hot wort into a fermenter containing 1½ gallons (6L) of chilled water. Top up to 5 gallons (19L).
3. Pitch yeast when cool.
4. Ferment at ale temperatures (65° to 70°F, 18° to 21°C).
5. Bottle when fermentation stops (2–3 weeks). Age 3 weeks before drinking.

EUROPEAN LAGERS

Bohemian Pilsner and Netherlands export lager are two common European lagers.

Bohemian Pilsner

Czechoslovakian or Bohemian Pilsner is the style of which most modern lager beers are pale imitations. The original is light-amber-colored, maltier, and less bitter than its German cousin, with a delicate aroma of honey. Bohemian Pilsner is nothing like its many American counterparts and really has to be tasted to be appreciated. Budvar and Pilsner Urquell are commercial examples of the style.

 **BOW ROCK PILSNER**

INITIAL GRAVITY: 1.050–1.055   FINAL GRAVITY: 1.014–1.016

    3 pounds Brewmart Czechoslovakian Pilsner kit (1.4 kg)
    2 pounds Dutch extra light dry malt extract (.9 kg)
    ½ ounce Saaz hop pellets for flavoring (14 g)
    ½ ounce Saaz hop pellets for aroma (14 g)
       Yeastlab European lager
    ¾ cup corn sugar for priming (180 ml)

1. Bring 1½ gallons (6L) of water to a boil. Add the extracts and boil the mixture for 20 minutes. Add ½ ounce (14 g) Saaz hop pellets to the last 10 minutes of boil. Add ½ ounce (14 g) Saaz hop pellets to the final 3 minutes of boil.
2. Strain hot wort into a fermenter containing 1½ gallons (6L) of chilled water. Top up to 5 gallons (19L).
3. Pitch yeast when cool.
4. Ferment at lager temperatures (40° to 50°F, 4° to 10°C).
5. Bottle when fermentation is complete (3–6 weeks). Age 4 weeks at lager temperatures.

COFFEEHOUSE BOHO PILSNER

INITIAL GRAVITY: 1.055–1.059   FINAL GRAVITY: 1.016–1.019

- ½ pound Cara-Pils malt (220 g)
- ½ pound Munich malt (220 g)
- 6.6 pounds Glen Brew Pilsner kit (3 kg)
- ½ ounce Saaz hop plug for flavoring (14 g)
- ½ ounce Saaz hop plug for bittering (14 g)
- Yeastlab L31 Pilsner
- ¾ cup corn sugar for priming (180 ml)

1. Add crushed grains to 1½ gallons (6L) of cold water and bring the mixture to a boil. Add the extract and return the mixture to a boil. Add ½ ounce (14 g) Saaz hop plug and boil for 20 minutes. Add ½ ounce (14 g) Saaz hop plug to the final 2 minutes of boil.
2. Strain hot wort into a fermenter containing 1½ gallons (6L) of chilled water. Top up to 5 gallons (19L).
3. Pitch yeast when cool.
4. Ferment at lager temperatures (40° to 50°F, 4° to 10°C).
5. Bottle when fermentation ceases (6–8 weeks). Age at lager temperatures for 4 weeks.

Netherlands Export Lager

Holland is one of several brewing nations that makes a beer specifically for export to the American market. Netherlands export is little like the beers the Dutch drink at home; it has increased amounts of adjuncts and less hops, as well as being brewed from a lower specific gravity.

TILL EULENSPIEGEL'S MERRY PRANK LAGER-ALE

This brew can be fermented as either a lager or an ale, depending on what yeast is used. Just remember to give it the appropriate temperature range.

INITIAL GRAVITY: 1.043–1.051   FINAL GRAVITY: 1.012–1.014

- 4 pounds Laaglander Light Lager kit (1.8 kg)
- 2 pounds Dutch extra light dry malt extract (.9 kg)
- ½ ounce Hallertau hop plug for flavoring (14 g)
- ½ ounce Hallertau hop plug for aroma (14 g)
- Yeastlab A07 Canadian ale or Wyeast #2042 Danish lager
- 1 cup corn sugar for priming (240 ml)

1. Bring 1½ gallons (6L) of water to a boil. Add the extracts and boil for 20 minutes. Add ½ ounce (14 g) Hallertau flavoring hops to the final 5 minutes of boil. Add Hallertau aroma hops to the final 2 minutes of boil.
2. Strain hot wort into a fermenter containing 1½ gallons (6L) of chilled water. Rinse hops with boiled water. Add water to make up 5 gallons (19L).
3. Pitch yeast when cool.
4. Ferment at cool ale temperatures (60° to 68°F, 16° to 20°C).
5. Bottle when fermentation ceases (2–4 weeks). Age cold (40° to 50°F, 4° to 10°C) for 4 weeks.

BILLIKENS EXPORT LAGER ALE

This is a more authentic rendition of Heineken, since it uses flaked maize as an adjunct.

INITIAL GRAVITY: 1.042–1.052   FINAL GRAVITY: 1.014–1.021

- ½ pound 3° Lovibond German crystal malt (220 g)
- ½ pound flaked maize (220 g)
- ¼ pound Cara-Pils (110 g)
- 4 pounds Laaglander Light Lager kit (1.8 kg)
- 1 pound Dutch extra light dry malt extract (.45 kg)
- 1 pound honey (.45 kg)
- 1 teaspoon Irish moss (5 ml)
- ½ ounce Hallertau hops for flavoring (14 g)
- ½ ounce Hallertau hops for aroma (14 g)
- Yeastlab A07 Canadian ale yeast
- ¾ cup corn sugar for priming (180 ml)

1. Hydrate the Irish moss in 1 cup (240 ml) of water overnight, or up to 8 hours.
2. Put the grains in a grain bag and add the bag to 1½ gallons (6L) of cold water. Bring the water to a slow boil over 30 minutes. Strain out the grains and rinse with ½ gallon (2L) of boiled water. Add the extracts, honey, and Irish moss and boil for 30 minutes. Add ½ ounce (14 g) Hallertau flavoring hops to the final 5 minutes of boil. Add ½ ounce (14 g) Hallertau aroma hops to the final 2 minutes of boil.
3. Strain hot wort into a fermenter containing 1½ gallons (6L) of chilled water. Rinse hops with boiled water. Add enough water to make up 5 gallons (19L).
4. Pitch yeast when cool.
5. Ferment at cool ale temperatures (60° to 68°F, 16° to 20°C).
6. Bottle when fermentation ceases (2–4 weeks). Age cold (40° to 50°F, 4° to 10°C) for 4 weeks before drinking.

GERMAN ALES

Among German ales are alts and weizenbeers (wheat ales).

Alt

Alt is a style of ale brewed in Düsseldorf. It is copper-colored, very bitter, and smooth, with some fruitiness, and is of medium alcoholic strength. Alt means "old," and the style and its method of warm fermentation are said to be older than the cold-fermented lagers for which Germany is known. Unlike British ales, both alt and Kölsch (see below) are fermented warm and then lagered cold.

 OY! GEV ALT

INITIAL GRAVITY: 1.045–1.050   FINAL GRAVITY: 1.016–1.019

- 3.5 pounds Geordie Mild kit (1.6 kg)
- 2 pounds dark dry malt extract (.9 kg)
- 1 ounce Perle hop pellets for bittering(28 g)
- 2 packets Doric ale yeast
- ¾ cup corn sugar for priming (180 ml)

1. Bring 1½ gallons (6L) of cold water to a boil. Add the extracts and return the mixture to a boil. Add Perle hop pellets and continue boiling for 45 minutes.
2. Strain hot wort into a fermenter containing 1½ gallons (6L) of chilled water. Top up to 5 gallons (19L).
3. Pitch yeast when cool.
4. Ferment at ale temperatures (65° to 70°F, 18° to 21°C).
5. Bottle when fermentation stops (7–10 days). Age 4 weeks at lager temperatures (40° to 50°F, 4° to 10°C).

BETTY'S LOBSTER QUADRILLE ALT

INITIAL GRAVITY: 1.044–1.050   FINAL GRAVITY: 1.014–1.019

- ½ pound Munich malt (220 g)
- ½ pound 40° Lovibond German crystal malt (220 g)
- 4 pounds Mountmellick Brown Ale kit (1.8 kg)
- 2 pounds Dutch dry amber malt extract (.9 kg)
- 1 ounce Chinook hop plug for bittering (14 g)
- ½ ounce Tettnang hop pellets for aroma (14 g)
- Wyeast #2565 Kölsch yeast
- ¾ cup corn sugar (180 ml) or 1¼ cups dry malt extract for priming (303 ml)

1. Three days before brewing, activate the yeast.
2. Put the crushed grains in a grain bag and add to 1½ gallons (6L) of cold water. Bring the water to a slow boil over 30 minutes. Strain out the grains and rinse with ½ gallon (2L) of boiled water. Add the extracts and return the mixture to a boil. Add Chinook bittering hops and boil for 60 minutes. Add Tettnang hop pellets to the final 3 minutes of boil. Steep for 5 minutes.
3. Strain hot wort into a fermenter containing 1½ gallons (6L) of chilled water. Top up to 5 gallons (19L).
4. Pitch yeast when cool.
5. Ferment at ale temperatures (65° to 70°F, 18° to 21°C). When primary fermentation slows, rack to secondary fermenter and lager at cool temperatures (40° to 50°F, 4° to 10°C) for 6–8 weeks.
6. Bottle when fermentation ceases. Age 4 weeks at lager temperatures before drinking.

Kölsch

Kölsch is a pale, light, dry, fruity ale with some hoppiness. It is brewed in the city of Cologne, Germany.

 **RHEINGOLD KÖLSCH**

INITIAL GRAVITY: 1.038–1.040   FINAL GRAVITY: 1.016–1.018

- 3.3 pounds John Bull Lager kit (1.5 kg)
- 2 pounds Dutch extra light dry malt extract (.9 kg)
- 1 teaspoon Irish moss (5 ml)
- 1 ounce German Hallertau hop pellets for bittering (28 g)
- 1–2 packets Doric ale yeast
- ¾ cup corn sugar for priming (180 ml)

1. Hydrate the Irish moss in 1 cup (240 ml) water overnight.
2. Bring 1½ gallons (6L) of cold water to a boil. Add the extracts and Irish moss and return the mixture to a boil. Add German Hallertau hop pellets and boil for 45 minutes. Strain hot wort into a fermenter containing 1½ gallons (6L) of chilled water. Top up to 5 gallons (19L).
3. Pitch yeast when cool.
4. Ferment at ale temperatures (65° to 70°F, 18° to 21°C).
5. Bottle when fermentation stops (7–10 days). Age 4 weeks at lager temperatures before drinking (40° to 50°F, 4° to 10°C).

KOENIG'S KÖLSCH

INITIAL GRAVITY: 1.040–1.044   FINAL GRAVITY: 1.016–1.020

1 pound Vienna malt (.45 kg)
½ pound 40° Lovibond German crystal malt (220 g)
1 teaspoon gypsum (5 ml)
3.5 pounds Geordie Lager kit (1.6 kg)
2 pounds Dutch plain light dry malt extract (.9 kg)
1 teaspoon Irish moss (5 ml)
1 ounce Perle hop plug for bittering (28 g)
½ ounce Liberty hop plug for flavoring (14 g)
Wyeast #2565 Kölsch yeast or
Yeastlab A06 Düsseldorf ale yeast
¾ cup corn sugar for priming (180 ml)

1. Three days before brewing, activate the yeast pack.
2. Hydrate the Irish moss overnight, or up to 8 hours.
3. Put the crushed grains in a grain bag. Add the grains and gypsum to 1½ gallons (6L) of cold water and bring to a slow boil over 30 minutes. Strain out the grains and rinse with ½ gallon (2L) of boiled water. Add extract and Irish moss. Return the mixture to a boil, add Perle hop plugs and continue boiling for 60 minutes. Add Liberty flavoring hops to the last 5 minutes of boil.
4. Strain hot wort into a fermenter containing 1½ gallons (6L) of chilled water. Rinse hops with boiled water. Top up to 5 gallons (19L).
5. Pitch yeast when cool.
6. Ferment at ale temperatures (65° to 70°F, 18° to 21°C). When primary fermentation slows, rack to secondary fermenter and lager at cool temperatures (40° to 50°F, 4° to 10°C) for 6–8 weeks.
7. Bottle when fermentation ceases. Age at lager temperatures for 4 weeks before drinking.

Weizenbier

Weizen, or weiss, is an unusual style of wheat ale from Bavaria. It is copper-colored, medium-bodied, and lightly hopped. The use of wheat and a distinctive yeast strain contribute both sourness and a spicy clove flavor to these beers. Both dunkel (dark) and helles (light) versions are brewed, along with a more alcoholic weizenbock.

 **WOOZY WEIZEN**

INITIAL GRAVITY: 1.050–1.055   FINAL GRAVITY: 1.014–1.018

   4 pounds Ironmaster Wheat kit (1.8 kg)
   2 pounds dry wheat extract (.9 kg)
     Yeastlab WSI Bavarian weizen
   ⅞ cup corn sugar for priming (210 ml)

1. Bring 1½ gallons (6L) of cold water to a boil. Add the extracts, return the mixture to a boil, and boil for 20 minutes.
2. Pour hot wort into a fermenter containing 1½ gallons (6L) of cold water. Top up to 5 gallons (19L).
3. Pitch yeast when cool.
4. Ferment at ale temperatures (65° to 70°F, 18° to 21°C).
5. Bottle when fermentation ceases (1–2 weeks). Age 3 weeks before drinking.

BIG TROUBLE BOB'S WEISSBOCK

INITIAL GRAVITY: 1.065–1.072   FINAL GRAVITY: 1.016–1.020

- 1 pound Quaker's Multigrain cereal (.45 kg)
- ¾ pound wheat malt (340 g)
- ¼ pound 40° Lovibond German crystal malt (110 g)
- 4 pounds Laaglander Light Dutch Lager kit (1.8 kg)
- 3.3 pounds Munton & Fison malt/wheat extract syrup (1.5 kg)
- 2 ounces Hallertau hops for bittering (57 g)
- ½ ounce Saaz hop plug for flavoring (14 g)
  - Wyeast #3056 Bavarian weissen yeast
- ¾ cup corn sugar for priming (180 ml)

1. Three days before brewing, activate the yeast pack.
2. Add the crushed grains to 1½ gallons (6L) of cold water. Steep for 10 minutes. Bring the grains to a slow boil over 30 minutes. Strain out the grains and rinse with ½ gallon (2L) of boiled water. Add the extracts and return the mixture to a boil. Add Hallertau hops and boil for 60 minutes. Add Saaz flavoring hops to the final 15 minutes of boil.
3. Strain hot wort into a fermenter containing 1½ gallons (6L) of chilled water. Top up to 5 gallons (19L).
4. Pitch yeast when cool.
5. Ferment at ale temperatures (65° to 70°F, 18° to 21°C).
6. Bottle when fermentation ceases (7–10 days). Age 3 weeks before drinking.

GERMAN LAGERS

German lagers include bocks, Munich helles, Dortmunder exports, dunkels, German Pilsners, rauchbiers, schwarzbiers, and Viennas.

Bock

Bock is a sweet, malty, full-bodied lager that originated in Einbeck, Germany. It is the stout of the lager world, traditionally dark and thick, to be sipped contemplatively from enormous steins. There are many versions: pale hellesbock; maibock, which is consumed on May Day; dopplebock, an even more powerful version of bock; and eisbock, in which the finished beer is frozen (and the ice removed) to lower its water content and increase its strength.

 **WALK THE WALK BOCK**

Walk the Walk Bock is simple to brew, but it demands patience and long lagering. It's smooth and malty, with some hop bitterness and a slightly hoppy, licorice finish. A good-keeping beer. We kept a carboy of it in a cold room all one winter and just siphoned off a pitcherful whenever we felt like it.

INITIAL GRAVITY: 1.056–1.060   FINAL GRAVITY: 1.012–1.016

   7.5 pounds Black Rock Bock kit (2 cans) (3.4 kg)
   ½ teaspoon Irish moss (2 ml)
     Yeastlab European lager yeast
   ½ cup corn sugar (125 ml) or ¾ cup dry malt extract for priming (180 ml)

1. Hydrate the Irish moss for 8 hours in 1 cup (240 ml) of water.
2. Bring 1½ gallons (6L) of cold water to a boil. Add the extract and Irish moss and boil for 15 minutes.

3. Add hot wort to a fermenter containing 1½ gallons (6L) cold water. Top up to 5 gallons (19L).
4. Pitch yeast when cool.
5. Ferment at lager temperatures (40° to 50°F, 4° to 10°C) for 6–8 weeks.
6. Bottle when ready. Age 2 months or more at lager temperatures.

P.D.Q. BOCK

INITIAL GRAVITY: 1.060–1.068   FINAL GRAVITY: 1.016–1.018

  ¾ pound Munich malt (340 g)
  ½ pound 40° Lovibond German crystal malt (220 g)
  ½ pound chocolate malt (220 g)
7.5 pounds Black Rock Bock kit (2 cans) (3.4 kg)
  3 ounces Hallertau hops for bittering (85 g)
    Yeastlab L32 Bavarian lager or Yeastlab L33 Munich lager
  ½ cup corn sugar (125 ml) or ¾ cup dry malt extract for priming (180 ml)

1. Put crushed malts in a grain bag and add the bag to 1½ gallons (6L) of cold water. Bring the water to a slow boil over 30 minutes. Strain out the grains and rinse with ½ gallon (2L) of boiled water. Add the extract and return the mixture to a boil. Add Hallertau bittering hops and boil for 60 minutes.
2. Strain hot wort into a fermenter containing 1½ gallons (6L) of chilled water. Add water to make 5 gallons (19L).
3. Pitch yeast when cool.
4. Ferment at lager temperatures (40° to 50°F, 4° to 10°C).
5. Bottle when fermentation ceases (6–8 weeks). Age at lager temperatures 1–4 months before drinking.

Munich Helles

This is a malty, golden Bavarian lager that is lower in gravity and not quite as hoppy as a Pilsner. Helles (pale) is so named to distinguish it from the traditional Bavarian or Munich dark beer.

 **HELLES BELLES**

INITIAL GRAVITY: 1.046–1.050   FINAL GRAVITY: 1.014–1.018

   3.3 pounds Kwoffit Export Hofstar Lager kit (1.5 kg)
     2 pounds Dutch extra light dry malt extract (.9 kg)
    ¼ ounce Saaz hop pellets for flavoring (7 g)
    ¼ ounce Saaz hop pellets for aroma (7 g)
       Yeastlab European lager yeast
    ¾ cup corn sugar for priming (180 ml)

1. Bring 1½ gallons (6L) of cold water to a boil. Add the extracts, return the mixture to a boil, and boil for 20 minutes. Add ¼ ounce (7 g) Saaz hop pellets to the last 15 minutes of boil. Add ¼ ounce (7 g) Saaz hop pellets to the final 5 minutes of boil. Steep for 5 minutes.
2. Strain hot wort into a fermenter containing 1½ gallons (6L) of chilled water. Top up to 5 gallons (19L).
3. Pitch yeast when cool.
4. Ferment at lager temperatures (40° to 50°F, 4° to 10°C).
5. Bottle when fermentation stops (6–8 weeks). Age 6 weeks at lager temperatures.

BIERGARTEN HELLES

INITIAL GRAVITY: 1.048–1.054   FINAL GRAVITY: 1.016–1.019

- ¼ pound Cara-Pils malt (110 g)
- ¼ pound Munich malt (110 g)
- 3.3 pounds Cooper's Draught kit (1.5 kg)
- 2 pounds Dutch light dry malt extract (.9 kg)
- ½ ounce Saaz hop pellets (14 g)
- ½ ounce Tettnang hop pellets (14 g)
- Wyeast #2308 Munich lager
- ½ ounce Saaz hop plug for dry hopping (14 g)
- ¾ cup corn sugar for priming (180 ml)

1. Three days before brewing, activate the yeast pack.
2. Put the grains in a grain bag and add the bag to 1½ gallons (6L) of cold water. Bring the water to a slow boil over 30 minutes. Remove grain bag. Add the extracts and return the mixture to a boil. Add ½ ounce (14 g) Saaz hop pellets and boil for 20 minutes. Add ½ ounce (14 g) Tettnang hop pellets to the final 2 minutes of boil. Steep for 5 minutes.
3. Strain hot wort into a fermenter containing 1½ gallons (6L) of chilled water. Top up to 5 gallons (19L).
4. Pitch yeast when cool.
5. Ferment at lager temperatures (40° to 50°F, 4° to 10°C). When fermentation slows, rack to a secondary fermenter and add ½ ounce (14 g) Saaz dry hops in a hop bag.
6. Bottle when fermentation stops (6–8 weeks). Age 6 weeks at lager temperatures.

Dortmunder Export

This style of lager is associated with the city of Dortmund, Germany, although it's not necessarily brewed there. Less hoppy than German Pilsner and less malty than Munich helles, Dortmunder export is stronger than both, medium-bodied, and amber-colored.

DOC'S DORTMUNDER LAGER

INITIAL GRAVITY: 1.049–1.052   FINAL GRAVITY: 1.010–1.012

  6.6 pounds Glen Brew Dortmunder lager kit (3 kg)
  ½ ounce German Hallertau hop pellets for flavoring (14 g)
  ½ ounce German Hallertau hop pellets for aroma (14 g)
     Yeastlab European lager
  ¾ cup corn sugar for priming (180 ml)

1. Bring 1½ gallons (6L) of cold water to a boil. Add the extract, return the water to a boil, and boil for 20 minutes. Add ½ ounce (14 g) Hallertau flavoring hops to the last 12 minutes of boil. Add ½ ounce (14 g) Hallertau aroma hops to the last 3 minutes of boil.
2. Strain hot wort into a fermenter containing 1½ gallons (6L) of chilled water. Top up to 5 gallons (19L).
3. Pitch yeast when cool.
4. Ferment at lager temperatures (40° to 50°F, 4° to 10°C).
5. Bottle when fermentation ceases (6–8 weeks). Age 4 weeks at lager temperatures.

QUI DORT DORTMUNDER LAGER

INITIAL GRAVITY: 1.044–1.052   FINAL GRAVITY: 1.016–1.018

½ pound Ireks Munich malt (220 g)
½ pound aromatic malt (220 g)
½ pound biscuit malt (220 g)
6.6 pounds Glen Brew Dortmunder lager kit (3 kg)
½ ounce German Hallertau hop plug for flavoring (14 g)
½ ounce German Hallertau hop plug for aroma (14 g)
    Wyeast #2308 Munich lager yeast
¾ cup corn sugar for priming (180 ml)

1. Three days before brewing, activate the yeast pack.
2. Put the grains in a grain bag and add the bag to 1½ gallons (6L) of cold water. Bring the water to a slow boil over 30 minutes. Strain out the grains and rinse with ½ gallon (2L) of boiled water. Add the extract and return the mixture to a boil. Add ½ ounce (14 g) Hallertau hop plug and boil for 20 minutes. Add ½ ounce (14 g) Hallertau hop plug to the last 3 minutes of boil. Steep for 5 minutes.
3. Strain hot wort into a fermenter containing 1½ gallons (6L) of cold water. Rinse hops with boiled water. Top up to 5 gallons (19L).
4. Pitch yeast when cool.
5. Ferment at lager temperatures (40° to 50°F, 4° to 10°C).
6. Bottle when fermentation ceases (6–8 weeks). Age 4 weeks at lager temperatures.

Dunkel

Munich dark beer (*dunkel* means "dark") is a malty, amber-brown lager without much hop character. The beer gets its roasted, caramel-like character from a rich variety of malts. Like Munich helles, dunkel has a medium alcohol content.

 **BUCKSHI DACKLE DUNKEL**

Buckshi was the name of a dackle (dachshund) that was owned by a German actor and liked to drink dunkel. Salvator Bier was his favorite brand.

INITIAL GRAVITY: 1.045–1.058   FINAL GRAVITY: 1.014–1.018

> 4 pounds Laaglander Bock kit (1.8 kg)
> 2 pounds Laaglander plain amber malt extract syrup (.9 kg)
> 2 teaspoons calcium carbonate (10 ml)
> 1 ounce Liberty hop pellets for bittering (28 g)
>   Yeastlab European lager yeast
> ¾ cup corn sugar for priming (180 ml)

1. Bring 1½ gallons (6L) of cold water to a boil. Add the extracts and calcium carbonate and return the mixture to a boil. Add Liberty hop pellets and boil for 60 minutes.
2. Strain hot wort into a fermenter containing 1½ gallons (6L) of chilled water. Top up to 5 gallons (19L).
3. Pitch yeast when cool.
4. Ferment at lager temperatures (40° to 50°F, 4° to 10°C).
5. Bottle when fermentation ceases (4–6 weeks). Age 4 weeks at lager temperatures.

TURKADUCKLE DUNKEL

INITIAL GRAVITY: 1.049–1.062   FINAL GRAVITY: 1.018–1.021

- ½ pound 40° Lovibond German crystal malt (220 g)
- ¼ pound Munich malt (110 g)
- ¼ pound chocolate malt (110 g)
- 4 pounds Laaglander Bock kit (1.8 kg)
- 2 pounds Laaglander plain amber dry malt extract (.9 kg)
- 2 teaspoons calcium carbonate (10 ml)
- 1½ ounce Hallertau hop plug for flavoring (42 g)
- ¼ ounce Tettnang hop pellets for aroma (7 g)
- Wyeast #2308 Munich lager yeast
- ¾ cup corn sugar for priming (180 ml)

1. Three days before brewing, activate the yeast pack. Add the crushed grains and calcium carbonate to 1½ gallons (6L) of cold water and bring the water to a slow boil over 30 minutes. Strain out the grains and rinse with ½ gallon (2L) of boiled water. Add the extracts and boil for 25 minutes. Add 1½ ounce (14 g) Hallertau flavoring hops to the last 10 minutes of boil. Add ¼ ounce (7 g) Tettnang hop pellets to the last 2 minutes of boil.
2. Strain hot wort into a fermenter containing 1½ gallons (6L) of chilled water. Rinse hops with boiled water. Top up to 5 gallons (19L).
3. Pitch yeast when cool.
4. Ferment at lager temperatures (40° to 50°F, 4° to 10°C).
5. Bottle when fermentation ceases (4–6 weeks). Age 4 weeks at lager temperatures.

Märzen/Oktoberfest

Märzen is a malty, copper-colored, medium-bodied lager. It was traditionally made in March to be consumed at Oktoberfest, hence its other name. It is similar, but not identical, to Vienna-style lagers.

 **MÄDCHEN MÄRZEN**

INITIAL GRAVITY: 1.045–1.055   FINAL GRAVITY: 1.012–1.018

- 4 pounds Alexander's plain malt extract syrup (1.8 kg)
- 4 pounds Laaglander Dutch Light Lager kit (1.8 kg)
- ½ pound Malto-dextrine powder (220 g)
- ½ ounce Tettnang hop pellets for aroma (14 g)
  Yeastlab European lager yeast
- ¾ cup corn sugar for priming (180 ml)

1. Bring 1½ gallons (6L) of cold water to a boil. Add the extracts and Malto-dextrine powder, return the mixture to a boil, and boil for 20 minutes. Add Tettnang hop pellets to the final 5 minutes of boil.
2. Pour hot wort into a fermenter containing 1½ gallons (6L) of chilled water. Top up to 5 gallons (19L).
3. Pitch yeast when cool.
4. Ferment at lager temperatures (40° to 50°F, 4° to 10°C).
5. Bottle when fermentation ceases (4–6 weeks). Age 4 weeks before drinking.

KLEIN OTTO'S OKTOBERFEST

INITIAL GRAVITY: 1.054–1.059   FINAL GRAVITY: 1.011–1.017

- ½ pound German 60° Lovibond crystal malt (220 g)
- ½ pound Munich malt (220 g)
- ½ pound special roast malt (220 g)
- 2 ounces chocolate malt (57 g)
- 6.6 pounds Glen Brew Dortmunder lager kit (3 kg)
- ½ ounce Tettnang hops for flavoring (14 g)
- 1 ounce Saaz hops for aroma (28 g)
- Yeastlab L32 Bavarian lager
- ⅔ cup corn sugar (160 ml) or 1 cup dry malt extract for priming (240 ml)

1. Put the crushed grains in a grain bag and add the bag to 1½ gallons (6L) of cold water. Bring the water to a slow boil over 30 minutes. Strain out the grains and rinse with ½ gallon (6L) of boiled water. Add the extract, return the mixture to a boil, and boil for 20 minutes. Add Tettnang flavoring hops to the final 15 minutes of boil. Add Saaz aroma hops to the last 4 minutes of boil.
2. Strain hot wort into a fermenter containing 1½ gallons (6L) of chilled water. Rinse hops with boiled water. Add enough cold water to make up 5 gallons (19L).
3. Pitch yeast when cool.
4. Ferment at lager temperatures (40° to 50°F, 4° to 10°C).
5. Bottle when fermentation ceases (6–8 weeks). Age at lager temperatures 1–4 months before drinking.

German Pilsner

This is the German version of Czechoslovakian Pilsner lager. It differs from the Bohemian version in that it is lighter in body and color, drier, and more assertively hopped. The pure flavor of German beers comes from adherence to the *Reinheitsgebot*, a law that limits the ingredients allowed in beer to malt, hops, yeast, and water. Many of us have been converted to a life of beer hunting by that first clean sip of real draft Pils.

 **SCHNITZLEGRUBEN PILS**

INITIAL GRAVITY: 1.038–1.042   FINAL GRAVITY: 1.015–1.018

- 3.3 pounds Munton & Fison Pilsner kit (1.5 kg)
- 2 pounds Dutch plain light dry malt extract (.9 kg)
- ½ ounce Tettnang hop pellets for bittering (14 g)
- ½ ounce German Hallertau hop pellets for aroma (14 g)
  Yeastlab European lager yeast
- ¾ cup corn sugar for priming (180 ml)

1. Bring 1½ gallons (6L) of cold water to a boil. Add the extracts and return the water to a boil. Add Tettnang hop pellets and boil for 45 minutes. Add German Hallertau aroma hop pellets to last 3 minutes of boil.
2. Strain hot wort into a fermenter containing 1½ gallons (6L) of chilled water. Rinse hops with boiled water. Top up to make 5 gallons (19L).
3. Pitch yeast when cool.
4. Ferment at lager temperatures (40° to 50°F, 4° to 10°C).
5. Bottle when fermentation ceases (6–8 weeks). Age 2 months at lager temperatures.

MUNCHAUSEN'S MAD TAPSTER PILS

INITIAL GRAVITY: 1.045–1.050   FINAL GRAVITY: 1.016–1.019

- ¾ pound Pilsner malt (340 g)
- ¼ pound Vienna malt (110 g)
- 4 pounds Ironmaster European Pilsner kit (1.8 kg)
- 2 pounds Dutch extra light dry malt extract (.9 kg)
- 1½ ounces Saaz hop plugs for bittering (42 g)
- ½ ounce Saaz hop pellets for aroma (14 g)
- Yeastlab L31 Pilsner
- ¾ cup corn sugar for priming (180 ml)

1. Add crushed grains to 1½ gallons (6L) of cold water and bring the water to a slow boil over 30 minutes. Strain out the grains and rinse with ½ gallon (2L) of boiled water. Add the extracts and return the mixture to a boil. Add 1½ ounces (42 g) Saaz hop plugs and boil for 60 minutes. Add ½ ounce (14 g) Saaz aroma hops to the last 2 minutes of boil and steep for 5 minutes.
2. Strain hot wort into a fermenter containing 1½ gallons (6L) of chilled water. Rinse hops with boiled water. Top up to make 5 gallons (19L).
3. Pitch yeast when cool.
4. Ferment at lager temperatures (40° to 50°F, 4° to 10°C).
5. Bottle when fermentation ceases (6–8 weeks). Age 2 months at lager temperatures.

Rauchbier

Rauchbier is a smoky, dark lager brewed in the Franconia region of Germany, the most famous of which is Rauchenfels. This beer is made with beechwood-smoked malt grains, which import a woodsmoke flavor that varies from subtle to strong, depending on the producer. Smoked beer is an acquired taste, but it doesn't take long to acquire it! Rauchbier goes especially well with smoked foods.

 ### ROLF'S RAUCHBIER

This beer gets its smoky taste from "liquid smoke" rather than smoked grains.

INITIAL GRAVITY: 1.054–1.063   FINAL GRAVITY: 1.011–1.015

- 4 pounds Laaglander Dutch Dark Lager kit (1.8 kg)
- 2½ pounds Dutch amber dry malt extract (1.2 kg)
- 1 tablespoon Wright's Liquid Smoke (15 ml)
- ½ ounce Tettnang hop plug for aroma (14 g)
- Yeastlab European lager yeast
- ⅔ cup corn sugar (160 ml) or 1 cup dry malt extract for priming (240 ml)

1. Bring 1½ gallons (6L) of cold water to a boil. Add the extracts and liquid smoke and boil for 20 minutes. Add Tettnang aroma hops to the last 5 minutes of boil.
2. Strain hot wort into a fermenter containing 1½ gallons (6L) of chilled water. Rinse hops with boiled water. Add water to make 5 gallons (19L).
3. Pitch yeast when cool.
4. Ferment at lager temperatures (40° to 50°F, 4° to 10°C).
5. Bottle when fermentation ceases (4–6 weeks). Age 6 weeks to 2 months before drinking.

SMOKY JOE'S RAUCHBIER

INITIAL GRAVITY: 1.038–1.045   FINAL GRAVITY: 1.014–1.018

  1 pound smoked pale malt (.45 kg)

  ¾ pound Munich malt (340 g)

  ½ pound Cara-Pils malt (220 g)

  ½ pound 40° Lovibond German crystal malt (220 g)

  4 pounds Laaglander Dark Dutch Lager kit (1.8 kg)

2½ pounds Dutch amber dry malt extract (1.2 kg)

1½ ounces Hallertau hop plugs for bittering (42 g)

  ½ ounce Tettnang hop plug for aroma (14 g)

    Yeastlab L32 Bavarian lager yeast

  ⅔ cup corn sugar for priming (160 ml)

1. To smoke your own grains, soak mesquite, apple, or hickory wood chips overnight in water. Prepare a bed of coals in a barbecue grill, or start gas grill. Drain the chips and place them in an even layer over the coals. A small cake pan or Pyrex roasting pan can be used to hold the grains. Cover and smoke for 15–20 minutes. Allow the grains to cool.
2. Crush the grains and add them to 1½ gallons (6L) of cold water. Bring the water to a boil over 30 minutes. Strain out the grains and rinse with ½ gallon (2L) of boiled water. Add the extracts and return the mixture to a boil. Add Hallertau hop plugs and boil for 60 minutes. Add Tettnang hop plug to the final 2 minutes of boil. Steep for 5 minutes.
3. Strain hot wort into a fermenter containing 1½ gallons (6L) of cold water. Top up to 5 gallons (19L).
4. Pitch yeast when cool.
5. Ferment at lager temperatures (40° to 50°F, 4° to 10°C).
6. Bottle when fermentation ceases (6–8 weeks). Age 6 weeks to 2 months at lager temperatures before drinking.

Schwarzbier

Schwarzbier (black beer) is a mild, dark lager from Bavaria. It is light in body and alcohol, with medium bitterness, and not nearly as robust as its midnight color would suggest.

 ### SCHWARZ PETER'S SCHWARZBIER

INITIAL GRAVITY: 1.030–1.036   FINAL GRAVITY: 1.014–1.016

   3.3 pounds Premier Mild Ale kit (1.5 kg)
     2 pounds Dutch plain dark malt extract (.9 kg)
    ½ ounce Hallertau hop plug for flavoring (14 g)
    ¼ ounce Mt. Hood hop pellets for aroma (7 g)
         Yeastlab European lager yeast
    ¾ cup corn sugar for priming (180 ml)

1. Bring 1½ gallons (6L) of cold water to a boil. Add the extracts, return the mixture to a boil, add Hallertau hop plug, and boil for 20 minutes. Add Mt. Hood aroma hops to the final 3 minutes of boil. Steep for 5 minutes.
2. Strain hot wort into a fermenter containing 1½ gallons (6L) of cold water. Top up to 5 gallons (19L).
3. Pitch yeast when cool.
4. Ferment at lager temperatures (40° to 50°F, 4° to 10°C).
5. Bottle when fermentation ceases (6–8 weeks). Age 4–6 weeks at lager temperatures before drinking.

ARNOLD'S SCHWARZBIER

INITIAL GRAVITY: 1.036–1.040   FINAL GRAVITY: 1.014–1.019

½ pound 90° Lovibond German crystal malt (220 g)
⅛ pound chocolate malt (55 g)
3.3 pounds Premier Mild Ale kit (1.5 kg)
2 pounds Dutch plain amber malt extract (.9 kg)
½ ounce Liberty hop pellets for bittering (14 g)
¼ ounce Liberty hop pellets for aroma (7 g)
Yeastlab L32 Bavarian lager yeast
¾ cup corn sugar for priming (180 ml)

1. Add crushed grains to 1½ gallons (6L) of cold water and bring the water to a slow boil over 30 minutes. Strain out the grains and rinse with ½ gallon (2L) of boiled water. Add the extracts and return the mixture to a boil. Add ½ ounce (14 g) Liberty hop pellets and boil for 60 minutes. Add ¼ ounce (7 g) Liberty aroma hops to the final 2 minutes of boil. Steep for 5 minutes.
2. Strain hot wort into a fermenter containing 1½ gallons of cold water. Top up to 5 gallons.
3. Pitch yeast when cool.
4. Ferment at lager temperatures (40° to 50°F, 4° to 10°C).
5. Bottle when fermentation ceases (6–8 weeks). Age 4–6 weeks at lager temperatures before drinking.

Vienna

Vienna lager is the lost beer of Austria, all but extinct in its place of origin. Generally lumped together with Märzen/ Oktoberfest as a German amber lager, it is much more than that. Sweetly malty with a distinct hop bitterness, Vienna deserves wider recognition as a style. Today most commercial examples come from Mexico, where the style arrived long ago with immigrating Austrian brewers.

 **VIENNA IN THE SOKALO**

If you've never had a round, frosted mug of foamy cerveza in an open-air café on a warm, Mexican night, then it's way past time you did. In the meantime, try this darkish Vienna, reminiscent of Negra Modelo.

INITIAL GRAVITY: 1.040–1.053   FINAL GRAVITY: 1.014–1.018

> 4 pounds Laaglander Dutch Dark Lager kit (1.8 kg)
> 2.2 pounds Premier hopped malt extract (1 kg)
> ½ ounce Tettnang hop plug for aroma (14 g)
> Yeastlab European lager yeast
> ¾ cup corn sugar for priming (180 ml)

1. Bring 1½ gallons (6L) of cold water to a boil. Add the extracts and boil for 20 minutes. Add Tettnang hop plug to the last 5 minutes of boil. Steep for 5 minutes.
2. Strain hot wort into a fermenter containing 1½ gallons (6L) of chilled water. Top up to 5 gallons (19L).
3. Pitch yeast when cool.
4. Ferment at lager temperatures (40° to 50°F, 4° to 10°C).
5. Bottle when fermentation stops (4–6 weeks). Age 4 weeks at lager temperatures before drinking.

SOUTH O' THE BORDER VIENNA

INITIAL GRAVITY: 1.045–1.058   FINAL GRAVITY: 1.014–1.018

- ¼ pound German 40° Lovibond crystal malt (110 g)
- ¼ pound Cara-Pils malt (110 g)
- ¼ pound Munich malt (110 g)
- ¼ pound Vienna malt (110 g)
- 4 pounds Laaglander Dutch Dark Lager kit (1.8 kg)
- 2.2 pounds Premier hopped malt extract (1 kg)
- ½ ounce Hallertau hop plug for flavoring (14 g)
- ½ ounce Tettnang hop plug for aroma (14 g)
- Yeastlab European lager yeast or Wyeast #2308 Munich lager
- ¾ cup corn sugar for priming (180 ml)

1. Add crushed grains to 1½ gallons (6L) of cold water and bring the water to a slow boil over 30 minutes. Add the extracts and return the mixture to a boil. Add Hallertau hop plug and boil for 20 minutes. Add Tettnang hop plug to the last 5 minutes of boil. Steep for 5 minutes.
2. Strain hot wort into a fermenter containing 1½ gallons (6L) of chilled water. Rinse hops with boiled water. Top up to 5 gallons (19L).
3. Pitch yeast when cool.
4. Ferment at lager temperatures (40° to 50°F, 4° to 10°C).
5. Bottle when fermentation stops (6–8 weeks). Age 4 weeks at lager temperatures before drinking.

4

EQUIPMENT

THE AMOUNT OF EQUIPMENT available to the homebrewer is enormous and ever-growing. You can now spend thousands or tens of thousands of dollars equipping your own home microbrewery, but it is not necessary to go to such extremes if you just want to brew a tasty and consistent beer on a regular basis. Here is a list of equipment and materials that we have found useful for the basic brewer. You don't need it all, especially at first. Some of these items come in the basic equipment set, and some must be purchased separately. Everything here can add to the simplicity and success of homebrewing, and none of it is very expensive. Items usually included in basic equipment sets are denoted by a ✓. Those you might wish to add to your materials on hand are marked with a +.

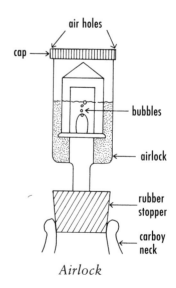

Airlock

✓ *Airlock.* The fermentation airlock can be used as a rough guide to the readiness of the beer. If bubbles have stopped coming out of the airlock, or if the interior plastic cylinder of an ale-style airlock is resting on its tube, then fermentation has ceased and it's time to

134

bottle. Also, if it takes 90 seconds or more for bubbles to appear, the beer is ready to bottle or keg.

+ *Blowby.* This is a simple system for venting sediments and carbon dioxide from your carboy. It consists of a stopper with a hole in it and a length of plastic tubing leading to a container that is partly filled with bleach water.

Once you have mastered the plastic fermenter bucket, you can move on to the blowby system, which is preferable for a number of reasons. The most important of these is that the blowby ejects much of the kraeusen that develops during primary fermentation. The kraeusen contains hop resins and other residues that can affect the quality of your beer. (This is especially true if you are brewing a light lager.)

Another reason for using this system is that some beers have very explosive primary fermentations, and residue can climb out of the fermentation lock or, worse yet, plug it. If you are using a carboy, the stopper can blow off and cause a hideous

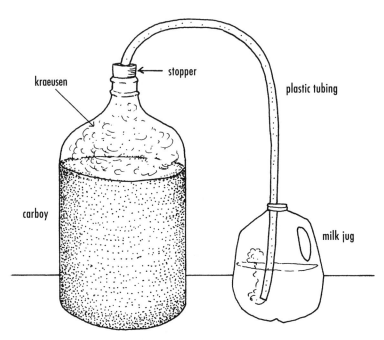

The blowby system

mess on the floor. (**Note:** This can also happen with the blowby, though it isn't as likely unless you are dry-hopping. Always keep an eye on the carboy during primary fermentation to prevent accidents.)

All you need is a 5½-gallon (21L) glass carboy, a #6½ rubber stopper with a hole in the center, a three-foot (.9 m) length of food-grade plastic tubing, and some kind of clean container half full of bleach water. We usually use a plastic milk jug, which lets us see when the bleach water needs to be changed.

To use the blowby system, brew your beer in the ordinary way, put the wort in the carboy, and pitch the yeast. (You will need a funnel to pour the wort into the carboy.) Now fit the sanitized plastic tube into the sanitized stopper and put it in the neck of the carboy. Carry the carboy to a quiet spot for fermentation and put the free end of the tube into the bleach solution in the milk jug. The whole thing forms an airlock.

As primary fermentation commences, the foamy kraeusen is pushed out of the tube by gas pressure and into the bleach-water container, along with a small amount of beer. This should be changed every day or so — more often if the fermentation is powerful and ejects a lot of matter. You should place some kind of tray under the container in case it overflows. After primary fermentation is complete, you can either rack to a bottling bucket (secondary fermenter) or just remove the tube and put a fermentation lock in the stopper to allow secondary fermentation to proceed in the same carboy.

The only problem we have ever had with this system occurred when the wort was too hot. When it cooled, it formed a vacuum inside the carboy and sucked bleach solution into the beer. To avoid this, you can put a fermentation lock in the stopper until the yeast gets going.

✓ *Bottle brush.* This is found in many equipment sets, or at a homebrew or hardware store. It is useful for cleaning bottles or scrubbing out the top of the carboy.

+ *Bottle washer.* This is hands-down the most time- and labor-saving device in the home brewery. It's a U-shaped brass valve that screws into a faucet. The end of the valve points up,

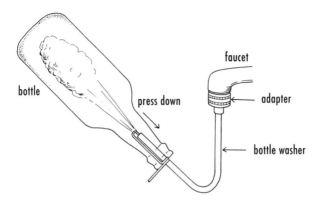

bottle

press down

faucet

adapter

bottle washer

Using a bottle washer

so you can invert a bottle or carboy, stick it over the top, and wash it out. These generally sell for less than $15, and the savings in hot water alone makes them worth the price. You can buy a separate adapter that will fit any faucet.

✓ *Bottling bucket/secondary fermenter.* The vessel in which the later stages of fermentation take place. You can begin by using the 5-gallon (19L) plastic bottling bucket with spigot that comes with the equipment set. In the case of beers that require a long secondary fermentation, such as bocks and barley-wine ales, it's a better idea to use a carboy. The food-grade plastic that the bottling bucket is made of is permeable to oxygen, which means that over an extended period of time oxygen molecules can pass right through it and into your beer. This is not a good idea because oxygen helps to break down beer.

+ *Brew pot.* This is used to boil the malt extract and other ingredients together with water. Some commercial stainless-steel brew pots we have seen have very thin bottoms, making it easy to burn the extract. So, if you plan to do a lot of brewing, it's a good idea to invest in a solid 16- to 20-quart stockpot. Revere Ware is an excellent, if expensive, brand. Sometimes you can get a good deal on a stockpot at kitchen outlet stores or restaurant supply stores.

For more advanced brewing, you'll need two brew pots, one to steep the grains and one to boil the wort. It's much easier to strain the sweet liquor from one pot to the other than it is to try to scoop out the grains.

✓*Capper.* A simple mechanical device for fixing metal caps firmly on beer bottles. Remember: You will need a bottle opener to remove them. Caps should also be included with your equipment set.

+ *Carboy.* A great advantage that carboys have over the plastic bucket is the fact that they're transparent. You can look through and see what your yeast is doing. It's very easy to tell where the end of your siphoning tube is and avoid sucking up the sediment. However, ultraviolet light can also pass through the sides of the carboy and make the beer "skunky," so it's a good idea to cover the carboy with something that will screen out the light. A black plastic trash bag or a coat will do fine.

Unlike plastic fermenters, carboys are easy to get really clean and sanitized. A carboy that has been used for brewing will have all kinds of proteins, yeast gunk, and wort sediment around the neck. It is easy to clean this out using a bottle brush and baking soda. A brass bottle washer is invaluable for rinsing out the carboy. Just invert it over the sink and rinse it like a big bottle. To sanitize the carboy, fill it up to the top with bleach solution and leave it overnight. When you are ready to brew, just pour out the bleach solution and rinse the carboy with hot water.

Carboys have another advantage over plastic fermenters: They are impermeable to oxygen, which means that oxygen molecules in the air cannot pass through them and into your beer. This only becomes a problem with plastic fermenters if you use them for long secondary fermentation or lagering. If you intend to make a lot of lagers, it's a good idea to do your secondary fermentation in a carboy.

Also, it's difficult to scratch carboys and make a place for bacteria to grow, which can easily happen with a plastic fermenter. Unless you drop a carboy or expose it to heat stress, it will last for years, so avoid pouring hot wort into a cold, empty carboy, or it might crack. If you always pour a gallon of cold water into the bottom of the carboy before adding wort, you shouldn't have this problem.

Most brew supply stores carry plastic-coated metal carboy handles. These can be attached easily with an adjustable wrench, and they make it much easier and safer to carry a full carboy. Wooden boxes that fit snugly around the carboy are also available. These have the advantage of protecting the carboy while it is being carried. You can also use a milk crate for this purpose.

+ *Filler.* After bottling your first few batches of beer, you will probably want to replace the filler wand. Plastic and brass models are available, but we prefer brass because they are very durable. When sanitizing any brass object, take care not to soak it too long in a bleach solution: It will discolor and begin to corrode.

✓ *Filler wand.* A plastic tube with a spring valve at one end that is used for filling beer bottles.

+ *Funnel.* A large plastic funnel is important when you start fermenting in a carboy.

+ *Grain bag.* A mesh bag in which grains are steeped, much like a giant tea bag. This makes controlling worts with a lot of grains, such as stout, much easier.

+ *Grain mill.* Most homebrew stores will have some kind of electric mill for crushing grain, so you can get it done right in the shop. You can also buy a home mill, such as the Philmill, but this is really only useful to all-grain brewers. Small amounts of grains can be crushed with a rolling pin or metal can. An easy way to do this is to put them inside a plastic freezer bag, lay the bag on a flat surface, and use the rolling pin or can to crack, rather than crush, the grains. Remember, they don't need to be ground too finely.

+ *Hop bag.* Similar to a grain bag. Used for confining dry hops in the bottling bucket.

✓ *Hydrometer.* A graduated glass instrument that measures the density — or specific gravity — of liquids as compared to water. The lower the specific gravity, the greater the alcohol content of your beer.

+ *Notebook.* A beer notebook is a vital resource. Use it to keep track of when you brewed, what ingredients you used, how long you boiled, how long the beer took to ferment, any problems you encountered, when you bottled, and how you liked the beer. Writing down your observations and procedures, as well as any questions that arise, will provide you with a record of your brewing progress and will allow you to reproduce any beers you especially liked or avoid problems in the future.

+ *Plastic bucket.* 5-gallon (19L) food-grade plastic buckets are useful for sanitizing bottles. They are available very cheaply from fast-food restaurants and other places that handle food in bulk. Don't use any that held pickles, vinegar, or jelly.

✓*Plastic tubing.* Clear plastic tubing is used to siphon beer, make the blowby, and connect the filler wand to the spigot of the bottling bucket. A short length comes with the equipment set. Eventually, even the best-cared-for blowby tube will discolor and turn an opaque, greenish color. When it does, retire it from the home brewery and get a new one.

✓*Primary fermenter.* The plastic 6-gallon (23L) bucket that comes with the equipment set. It's useful to have around even after you begin fermenting in carboys. It can hold sanitizing bottles, and it's always useful for holding that extra batch of fermenting beer.

+ *Spoon.* It can be metal or plastic, but it must have a long handle.

+ *Stopper.* You will need two rubber stoppers for your carboy: one with a hole in it to allow for the blowby tube and fermentation lock, and a solid one for those times when it's useful to stop the neck of the carboy, such as when chilling the wort. Both kinds are available at your homebrew store and come in standard sizes. A size 6½ stopper will fit snugly into most 5-gallon (19L) carboys.

+ *Strainer.* A metal strainer is useful for rinsing grains and straining spent hops from wort. It should fit inside the funnel (see above).

✓*Thermometer.* For measuring the temperature of the wort.

+ *Wine thief.* A plastic or glass tool used to take wort or finished beer from a fermenter. Mainly used when testing beer with a hydrometer.

+ *Wort chiller* (immersion type). A coil of copper tubing used to cool wort before pitching the yeast.

Cleaning and Sanitizing Materials

+ *Baking soda.* Sodium bicarbonate is an abrasive cleanser that is nontoxic to your beer and to yourself. It can be used to clean beer equipment such as scummy blowby tubes, carboys, and brew pots. Never use detergent to clean dirty beer equipment because the soapy residue it leaves behind is bad for beer. In an ideal world brew pots would be used only for brewing and would never come into contact with soap. If you occasionally use your brewpot for cooking lobsters, chili, or spaghetti sauce, it is a good idea to clean it out with baking soda before and after brewing.

+ *Bleach.* Chlorine bleach is a great sanitizing product for brewing. It is easy to handle, cheap, and safe to use. We use a solution of about ½ cup (125 ml) per 5 gallons (19L) of water for sanitizing bottles and equipment. Always use cold water in the solution because heat destroys the sanitizing properties of bleach. Remember: It is necessary to rinse the bottles thoroughly with hot water.

5

TIME TO ENJOY

ONCE YOU'VE MADE your first batch of beer, you'll want to serve it when it's at its peak of maturity and its most appropriate temperature. You'll also want to dispense it professionally. Here are some tips.

IS IT READY YET?

Beer should be served at its peak of maturity. This will vary depending on the style, hop rate, and alcohol content of the beer. In general, ales don't keep as well as lagers. Bitters, milds, and browns should be drunk young (2–6 weeks old). While a 6-week-old pale ale is in its prime, a 2-month-old pale ale has already begun to lose flavor. Bear in mind that some styles of ale, such as IPA and Russian Imperial stout, were designed to keep for a long time. Well-hopped and strongly alcoholic ales such as Trappist tripel and barley-wine ale, provided they are bottled with oxygen-absorbing caps, will last for years.

Lagers, on the other hand, generally improve with age, and even light lagers can be kept longer than ales. A 2-month-old light lager will be at its peak. Strong lagers such as Märzen and bock were designed to be drunk at least 6 months after brewing. Provided they are kept cold and out of the light, lagers store well and can be brewed in the cold winter months for enjoyment in summer.

WARM OR COLD?

The temperature at which beer should be served is a topic of some debate. American lagers are always served ice-cold, as close to 32°F (0°C) as possible. This is a good idea on a sweltering day in August, but what about in the depths of winter? An Irish stout served at 55°F (13°C) begins to sound very good indeed. The proper temperature for beer depends on such subjective factors as mood, season, style of beer, and whether you are eating anything with the beer. In general, temperature is a matter of taste. If the beer is too cold, you can't taste it. Many Americans recoil from "warm" British beer, but in reality no one serves beer warm. Ales are always served at cellar temperature. So are German lagers, and nobody ever accused the Germans of drinking warm beer.

POURING THE BEER

Homebrew is usually served in a glass because you don't want to drink the brown ooze in the bottom of the bottle. This is not bad for you — in fact, it's full of vitamins — but it isn't exactly appetizing either. Handle the bottle gently to avoid stirring up the sediment.

Remove the cap with a bottle opener and pour the beer all at once without setting it down. Pour slowly, tilting the glass to avoid building up too much of a foamy head, and then

How to pour a homebrew

level the glass for the last ½ inch (1.3 cm). Stop pouring when the sediment starts moving toward the neck of the bottle. With a little practice you will be able to pour out most of the beer, leaving only the sludgy sediment behind.

DESIGNING YOUR OWN BEER

Once you have been brewing for a while, it's fun to start designing your own recipes. This is one of the most rewarding aspects of homebrewing, and it is not as difficult as it sounds. As you brew the recipes in this book, you will soon get a feel for what different ingredients add to the finished product. You will develop preferences not only among beer styles, but among types of hops, yeast, and adjuncts.

Our recipes should be considered a basis for experimentation, and reasonable substitutions can be made for any of the ingredients. If you can't find a kit of a certain brand, feel free to use another one. If you like the flavor of a certain hop or the characteristics of a particular yeast, go ahead and use it. Beer recipes aren't graven in stone, and often small changes result in greatly improved beer.

When designing with kits, you may want to do a test batch of a particular kit as a control, to learn the characteristics of the basic recipe. Some kits can be used in a wide variety of styles, not just the one listed on the label.

6

TROUBLESHOOTING

IT GOES WITHOUT SAYING that your beer should taste good. If the recipe is sound, then the homebrewed product should be at least as savory and fresh as any store-bought brew. Obviously, if your beer is not first quality, then there is no reason to go to all the work of making it.

The point of this book is to ensure that your first attempt (and every effort after) comes out well. But if your ale or lager tastes, well, a little strange, don't bundle your equipment set into the closet and never look at it again. Trust us; there is a reason for every failed batch, and usually it's something simple and preventable. Here are some of the most common problems associated with basic brewing.

WHY DIDN'T MY YEAST START?

This is the single most common problem that new brewers call their homebrew stores to ask about. It means that, after pitching, the yeast never shows any activity, such as bubbling, foaming, and throwing off carbon dioxide, to indicate that it is still alive. Sometimes their panic is premature, particularly in the case of liquid yeasts, which are notorious for slow starts.

If there are no bubbles coming out of the airlock, open the fermenter lid and check the yeast. If it is active, it's possible that the fermenter leaks, and CO_2 is escaping from somewhere other than the airlock. But sometimes the yeast really is dead, and there are only three reasons for it.

- ◆ *The pitching temperature was too hot.* Yeasts, as we have said earlier, really are very delicate organisms. Temperatures that might seem comfortable to a human being can be lethal to a one-celled organism like yeast. While it is very difficult to kill yeast with cold (they become dormant), it is easy to kill them with heat. With experience, you will be able to tell the correct pitching temperature, but until you become experienced, always take a temperature reading before pitching. Repitching with fresh yeast after the wort has cooled will save your brew.
- ◆ *The sanitizing solution remained in the fermenter.* If your fermenter was not completely rinsed out with hot water, the sterilant used to kill harmful microorganisms on its surface could also kill the yeast. In this case, repitching won't help you. Throw out the batch and try again.
- ◆ *The yeast was dead to begin with.* Pitch again, this time with fresh yeast.

WHY DID MY YEAST STOP WORKING?

This is the second most common problem that new brewers call about. If the recipe says that fermentation should take a week to 10 days, yet all activity has ceased after 48 hours, it may not be a problem. Some yeasts are faster than others, especially at higher fermentation temperatures. If your yeast has stopped, take a hydrometer reading. If it is within the final gravity range for your recipe, go ahead and bottle. If not, see the next question.

WHAT IS STUCK FERMENTATION? WHAT CAN I DO ABOUT IT?

A "stuck" fermentation is one in which the specific gravity is higher than you would expect it to be, yet the yeast has already stopped working. In kit brewing, this may be caused by unfermentable *dextrins* added to the malt extract to enhance body. With experience you will be able to tell by looking whether the fermentation is complete.

Aeration of the wort, variety, and amount of yeast pitched sometimes make a difference in the final attenuation of the beer. Trust your yeast and bottle when fermentation ceases. However, if the yeast stops working and the hydrometer reading seems wrong, move your beer to a warmer place and wait a week before taking another reading. If your reading is still too high, there are a few things you can do. Yeast nutrient, an ingredient used in wine making, is available at your homebrew store. Sometimes a tablespoon or so added to the fermenter can revive sluggish yeasts. As a last resort, you can try pitching again with a more attenuative yeast. Sometimes in the case of highly alcoholic beers such as barley-wine ale, the yeast produces so much alcohol that it is unable to continue fermenting, and it drops out of solution.

WHAT CAUSES THE FAINT HAZINESS ON MY COLD BEER?

This is called a "chill haze." It is not much of a problem in dark beers, but if it bothers you in your lighter beers, it can be avoided easily. Chill haze can be caused either by proteins in the beer or by bacterial infection. In the latter case, better sanitization will clear it up. If protein is your problem, chilling the water in your primary fermenter before adding the hot wort should help. This will encourage a good cold break, which will eliminate extra proteins in your brew.

WHY IS MY BEER CLOUDY?

Some beers, like Witbier, are supposed to be cloudy, but usually cloudiness, like haziness and beads of matter around the top of the bottle, is a good indication of infected beer. Go back and clean your bottles.

THERE'S FOREIGN MATTER FLOATING IN MY BEER. SHOULD I BE CONCERNED?

Most often, when a new brewer calls the supply store with this problem, it's not a problem. Top-fermenting ale yeasts, especially if they are kept in a warm place, will rise to the surface of the bottle during carbonation to eat the priming sugar. Any brewer can be frightened by this, so open a bottle and taste it. If it tastes fine, chances are it isn't infected. However, if your beer has already carbonated and has been sitting in the cellar for months, it's possible that you really have an infection. Strange growths in your beer are the result of unclean equipment and poor sanitation. No known disease microorganisms can live in beer because of its alcohol content and acidity. However, if your beer starts sprouting polyps, take no chances and toss it on the compost. Then carefully sanitize your bottles and all your equipment. While you're at it, wipe all the surfaces in your brewery with a rag dampened with bleach water. You'll be glad you did.

WHY DOES MY BEER HAVE A CIDERY TASTE?

There are not many reasons why you might have cider-flavored beer. One is the use of corn sugar or cane sugar in your brewing. If you are using our recipes, you shouldn't be having this problem. Another reason you might have cidery flavors is the yeast you used. Sometimes yeast packets that come with kits have been left unrefrigerated for a long time. Sometimes they are not microbiologically pure. And sometimes a yeast will just produce unpleasant flavors. Use a fresh, healthy yeast that has been kept refrigerated, and you can avoid this problem.

The primary reason you may have cidery or otherwise undesirable flavors in your beer is bacterial or wild yeast infection. Keep your bottles and equipment sanitized, brew clean, and you'll keep infections to a minimum.

MY LATEST BATCH HAD AN ODD FLAVOR. WHAT MIGHT CAUSE THAT?

Sometimes unusual ingredients can contribute new — or even strange — flavors. Wheat and rye malts can open up new worlds of taste. Some yeasts, such as Whitbread and Ringwood ale yeasts, have distinctive flavors of their own. And brewing with spices, such as ginger, cinnamon, and coriander, can be a shock to the taste buds of a novice. If you haven't added anything but malt extract and hops, you may have an infection. Careful sanitation will prevent many of these problems. (See "Sanitation, Again" box below.)

HOW CAN I PREVENT MY BEER FROM TASTING SOUR?

Sour flavors are the result of either overhopping or wild-yeast infection. Some beers, notably wheat beers and lambics, are supposed to be sour. If your beer is overhopped, put it back in the cellar for a few more weeks, and it will smooth out. If you have wild yeasts, you need better sanitation procedures. (See "Sanitation, Again" box, page 149.)

WHY DOES THE HEAD ON MY BEER DISAPPEAR?

Poor head retention is just a result of soapy glassware. Waxes and soap residues break down the foamy head. This is the reason bartenders are constantly rinsing their beer glasses.

SANITATION, AGAIN

Breweries have to maintain near-operating-room cleanliness. While you can't go to that extreme, you need to keep your home brewery as free as possible from contaminating organisms. Always run a rag soaked in bleach water around the brewing area before and after you brew. Bugs that love wort will build up in this area over time, so it's important to keep their populations low by scrupulous cleaning.

Rinsing out glasses just before serving the beer should help with this problem. The use of very fresh hops in the brew pot also will help, as would a judicious addition of wheat or Cara-Pils malt in a complex brew such as stout or porter.

HOW CAN I AVOID OVERCARBONATING MY BEER?

Excessive carbonation is usually the result of overpriming or bottling a beer that is not completely fermented. To carbonate 5 gallons (19L) of beer, ¾ cup (180 ml) of corn sugar or 1¼ cups (295 ml) of dry malt extract is sufficient. However, yeast can digest the dark malts used in beers such as stout and porter, so these beers should always be primed with less sugar (½ cup [125 ml] of corn sugar or ¾ cup [180 ml] of dry malt extract) to avoid overcarbonation. A wild-yeast infection can also cause overcarbonation, so be careful with sanitation. (See "Sanitation, Again" box, page 149.)

WHY DOES MY BEER HAVE NO CARBONATION?

Lack of carbonation can be a sign of underpriming, or storing beer where the temperature is too low. Move the beer to a warmer location and wait a week. If it's still flat, it may be that you failed to rinse all of the sterilant out of your bottles, and it killed the yeast. Perhaps an infection has outcompeted your yeast and eaten the priming sugar. You *did* add priming sugar, didn't you? As a last resort, try uncapping the bottles and adding a few grains of new yeast, or ¼ teaspoon (1 ml) corn sugar, to each bottle and recap.

Some styles, like most English ales and some wheat beers, are intentionally low in carbonation, so the lack of a huge, foamy head is not a problem. High-alcohol brews such as dopplebock, some stouts, and Trappist tripel take longer than usual to carbonate, and most of these beers need to be aged a long time before drinking, anyway. It takes a while for their robust characters to develop and mature.

GLOSSARY

Adjuncts. Fermentable beer ingredients other than malted barley. Includes corn, rice, wheat, oats, and rye.

Aerobic. Processes requiring oxygen. Includes the respiration phase of fermentation.

Ale. Style of beer produced by top-fermenting yeast strains at warm temperatures that originated in the British Isles. Includes bitter, stout, porter, India Pale, and others.

Alpha acids. The acids that form the main bittering agents in hops.

Anaerobic. Processes that do not require oxygen, such as fermentation and flocculation.

Aroma. The characteristic smell of beer, sometimes called "nose," that is produced by malt, hops, and yeast.

Attenuation. The difference between initial specific gravity and final gravity, which indicates the amount of dissolved sugars converted by yeast into alcohol and carbon dioxide.

Barley. A cereal grain, the seeds of which (barleycorns) are used in making beer. Different varieties — 2-row and 6-row — impart different qualities to the beer.

Beta acids. Secondary bittering acids of hops.

Body. The consistency or texture of beer, sometimes called "mouth feel," that is described as light, medium, or full.

Carboy. A 5- to 6½-gallon, clear-glass bottle that can be used as a fermenting vessel.

Cold break. The stage during the cooling of hot wort when proteins precipitate as "trub."

Conditioning. The stage during beer aging when carbonation develops.

Dextrins. Unfermentable elements that contribute body to beer.

Ester. Organic compounds that contribute fruitlike flavors to beer.

Fermentation. The stage of the yeast's life cycle following reproduction during which it eats and then produces alcohol, carbon dioxide, and some of the flavors of beer.

Fermentation lock. The plastic valve that vents carbon dioxide from the fermentation vessel and prevents contamination of beer by microbes.

Fining agent. An ingredient such as gelatin, Irish moss, or isinglass that is used to clarify beer.

Finishing hops. Hops that are added at the end of the boil to contribute delicate hop aromas to the beer. (They are also called aroma hops.) Hallertau, Saaz, and Willamette are three varieties often used as finishing hops.

Flocculation. The stage of fermentation during which yeast clumps together and either migrates to the top (top-fermenting yeast) or settles to the bottom (bottom-fermenting yeast) of the fermentation vessel. Beer in which the yeast has undergone flocculation is said to have "dropped clear."

HBU. Homebrew bitterness units, a measure of the bitterness potential of a particular kit for given volume of beer.

Hot break. The stage in the process of boiling the wort when proteins coagulate.

Hydrometer. A graduated glass instrument used to measure the specific gravity of liquids such as unfermented wort or finished beer.

Kraeusen. The high, foamy head produced on beer by primary fermentation.

Lager. A style of beer produced by bottom-fermenting yeasts at low temperatures. Originated in Germany, this style includes Märzens, bocks, and Oktoberfests.

Lautering. The process of straining sweet wort from spent grains following mashing.

Lovibond. A system of measuring beer color based on the color that 1 pound of malt will contribute to 1 gallon of beer. Recently replaced by Standard Reference Method (SRM).

Malt. A cereal grain (generally barley, but not always) that has been partially germinated, dried, and/or roasted to produce different brewing characteristics. Malt varieties include pale malt, crystal malt, black patent malt, chocolate malt, and Vienna malt.

Malt extract. Concentrated wort in syrup or powder form that may be hopped or unhopped.

Mashing. The process of extracting sweet liquor from malted grains by means of temperature-controlled steeping.

Pitching. Adding yeast to wort.

Primary fermentation. The very active first phase of fermentation that proceeds from the time of pitching until the kraeusen drops and includes the respiration and reproduction stages of the yeast's life cycle.

Primary fermenter. The vessel in which primary fermentation takes place. It can be either a 6½-gallon (24½L) plastic bucket or a carboy.

Priming. The process of adding sugar or malt extract to beer at bottling time to induce carbonation.

Racking. The process of siphoning unfinished homebrew from the primary fermentation vessel to the secondary fermentation vessel or bottling bucket.

Respiration. The aerobic process by which yeast absorbs oxygen for use during its life cycle.

Secondary fermentation. The less active, later stage of fermentation that proceeds from the time the kraeusen drops until the yeast flocculates out of solution and includes the fermentation and flocculation stages of the yeast's life cycle.

Secondary fermenter. The vessel in which secondary fermentation takes place. It can be a carboy or plastic bucket with spigot (bottling bucket).

Sparging. The process of rinsing residual sugars from mashed grains with boiled water.

Specific gravity. The density of a liquid as compared to water.

Standard Reference Method (SRM). The system of measuring beer color based on light refraction. SRM is approximately interchangeable with the older Lovibond system.

Sweet liquor. The liquid produced by all-grain mashing.

Sweet wort. Wort that has had no hops added.

Trub. Whitish protein scum that rises to the top of the brew kettle during boiling.

Wort. Unfermented beer.

Yeast. Microscopic plants that produce alcohol, carbon dioxide, and some of the flavors of beer through their life cycle. Lager yeasts *(Saccharomyces uvarum)*, generally bottom-fermenting, cold-tolerant, and slow-acting, produce few esters and characteristic yeast flavors. Ale yeasts *(Saccharomyces cerevisiae)*, generally top-fermenting and fast-acting, require warm temperatures to thrive, often produce esters, and have strong flavors of their own.

A

AMOUNTS AND CONVERSIONS

Three measuring systems — United States, Imperial (British), and Metric — confuse the homebrewing world. Here are a few basic rules to help you make sense of it all.

U.S.	METRIC	U.S.	METRIC
½ teaspoon	2 ml	*weight:*	
1 teaspoon	5 ml	¼ ounce	7 grams (g)
2 teaspoons	10 ml	½ ounce	14 g
3 teaspoons	15 ml	1 ounce	28 g
¼ cup	60 ml	¼ pound	110 g
⅓ cup	80 ml	½ pound	220 g
½ cup	120 ml	¾ pound	340 g
1 cup	240 ml	1 pound	450 g, .45 kg
2 cups (1 pint)	475 ml		(kilogram)
		1½ pounds	.7 kg
liquid measure:		2 pounds	.9 kg
½ gallon	2 litres (L)	3 pounds	1.4 kg
1 gallon	4L	3.3 pounds	1.5 kg
1½ gallons	6L	3.5 pounds	1.6 kg
2 gallons	7½L	4 pounds	1.8 kg
3 gallons	11½L	5 pounds	2.3 kg
4 gallons	15L	6 pounds	2.7 kg
5 gallons	19L	6.6 pounds	3 kg
6 gallons	23L		

temperature:

Degrees Celsius = 5/9 (F – 32)

Degrees Fahrenheit = (9/5 x C) + 32

length:	
1 inch	25 mm, 2½ cm

B

KEGGING THE CORNELIUS WAY

by Ben Gleason

Instead of bottling, try kegging your beer in a Cornelius kegging system (the old soda-tank dispensers). These systems usually include:

- *5-pound (2.3 kg) CO$_2$ tank.* This provides the carbonation for the beer and the pressure to dispense it.
- *Regulator (single- or double-gauge).* This unit allows the user to adjust the amount of CO$_2$ going into the keg. Turning the set screw clockwise increases the amount of CO$_2$, and vice versa. If two gauges are supplied with the regulator, one will read the amount of pressure going into the keg, and the other will indicate the amount of gas left in the CO$_2$ tank. A plastic crush washer is also included. This piece should go between the CO$_2$ tank and the regulator where they attach to one another.
- *5-gallon (19L) keg (pin- or ball-lock type).* This vessel holds the beer and comes in two basic types, determined by the style of the tank plugs (gas inlets and liquid outlets). Both styles are used by major soft-drink companies, so neither is superior.
- *Disconnects (pin- or ball-lock type).* These devices fit onto the tank plugs on the kegs. On pin-lock kegs the "gas in" side has two pins and the "beer out" side has three. With ball locks there is either a color code or the words "in" and "out" stamped in the appropriate places.
- *Tubing (food-grade vinyl).* Enough said.
- *Squeeze faucet.* Squeeze = beer ('til the keg runs out).
- *Hose clamps.* May or may not be included. They are a good safety idea. Use them at the end of each piece of tubing.

Using the Keg

1. *Sanitize the keg thoroughly.* This job is done best with commercially available sanitizing agents such as B-brite or Iodophor. Chlorine-based sanitizers (i.e., bleach) should be avoided as they can eat away at the stainless steel of the keg, forming pits or, eventually, holes in the metal. Apply CO_2 to the tank and squeeze the faucet to run sanitizer through the dip-tube and the liquid-out assembly (tank plug, liquid disconnect, tubing, and faucet). Rinse according to the type of the sanitizer.

NOTE: When sanitizing, check the various rubber O-rings. If they look dry, cracked, or especially flat, replace them. If they smell like soda, replace them.

2. *Siphon beer into the keg.* Enjoy a beer now! Once you were intimately involved in the lives of 48–50 bottles. Realize how much you don't miss them.

3. *Attach the keg lid.* Turn the CO_2 tank on. Attach the gas disconnect to the keg. Set the regulator screw to supply 8 pounds (3.6 kg) per square inch (6.5 sq cm) (psi). Check for leaks around the lid. If the keg is leaking at the lid, unhook the CO_2, reposition the lid slightly, and try again.

4. *Purge the keg of air.* This will lengthen the life of your beer and keep its quality high. Once the CO_2 has been on the beer for 20 seconds, pull the safety valve on the lid for 2 seconds. If the lid has no valve, remove the gas disconnect and depress the center of the gas tank plug for 2 seconds.

WARNING: Depress only the gas side; depressing the liquid side will provide you with a shower of your latest homebrew! Repeat this purging two more times. The keg is now free of air and the nasties that live in it.

5. *Carbonate the beer.* Leave the CO_2 connected and on (set at 8 pounds [3.6 kg] per square inch [6.5 sq cm]) for 5 days. Over this period CO_2 will dissolve into the beer — this is carbonation. At the end of 5 days remove the CO_2 and hide your beer so it can age to perfection.

NOTE: Carbonating at 8 pounds (3.6 kg) per square inch (6.5 sq cm) at 60°F (16°C) will result in a very low British-style carbonation. Fizzier beer takes more pressure and cooler temperatures.

6. *Serve the beer.* The moment you've been waiting for! Turn on the CO_2 tank. Attach the gas disconnect to the keg. Attach the liquid disconnect and faucet assembly to the keg. Turn the regulator screw to 12 pounds (5.4 kg) per square inch (6.5 sq cm). Squeeze the faucet. (The serving pressure is always more than the carbonating pressure, otherwise the CO_2 in the beer would be used up pushing the beer out of the keg, eventually leaving the beer flat.)

Emergency Quick Carbonation

Chill the filled and purged keg to 30° – 35°F (1° to 1.7°C). (Don't worry, it won't freeze.) Set the regulator to 30 pounds (14 kg) per square inch (6.5 sq cm). Shake the keg for approximately 30 seconds every 15 minutes for about 2 hours. After two hours the beer should be carbonated enough to serve.

NOTE: Reduce the pressure for dispensing the beer. (You'll have to experiment with this a bit.)

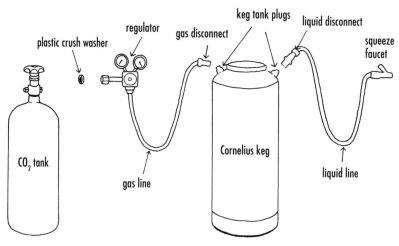

Cornelius kegging system

C

USING A WORT CHILLER

Chilling wort quickly is a vital step in the homebrewing process. It facilitates the cold break, reduces production of dimethyl sulfide, and permits timely yeast pitching. If nothing else, it lets you go to bed without worrying that your wort is sitting warm and yeastless. There are several types of devices available to accomplish this, but we will deal only with the immersion chiller.

The immersion wort chiller is designed for ease of use and efficient cooling. The water from your tap runs through the coil, picking up heat from the hot wort and carrying it away. Since no wort runs through the coil, you do not need to worry about sugars building up and forming a breeding ground for harmful bacteria.

Tips for Best Results

- Rinse the copper coil in a sanitizing solution (Iodophor, B-brite, Chempro, etc). Wash off the sterilant with warm tap water. Place the coil in the boiling wort for the last 15 minutes of the boil. This will complete the sterilization.
- At the end of the boil take the pot of hot wort — wort chiller and all — and place it near or in the sink. Attach one of the flexible tubes to the chiller and hook the other end to the sink faucet with the hardware provided. Attach one end of the remaining flexible hose to the other chiller opening. Place the outflow end of the tube in the drain.
- Turn on the cold-water tap. Cold water should flow at a rate that would allow a quart jar to be filled in approximately 20 seconds. This rate will allow the quickest cooling time. Two and one half gallons (10L) of just-boiled wort can be cooled in 15 minutes or less, depending somewhat

on the season and temperature of the tap water. Stirring gently with a sanitized spoon helps to facilitate cooling, but be sure not to introduce excessive air into the wort when it is still hot.

◆ When the wort is cool (80°F [27°C] or less), remove the chiller and proceed to strain hops, top up, and pitch the yeast. Wash the chiller well in a sanitizing solution and rinse, turning it upside down to drain the water in the coils before storing it.

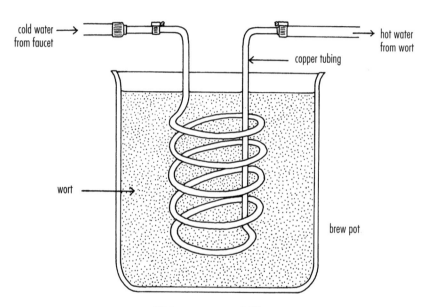

cold water → from faucet

hot water from wort

copper tubing

wort →

brew pot

Using a wort chiller

D

SELECTED BEER KIT SUPPLIERS

Not living near a brew store is no excuse not to brew; most of them now offer mail-order catalogs, and many have 800-numbers for in-state customers.

Alfred's Brewing Supply
P.O. Box 5070
Slidell, LA 70469
(504) 641-2545

Bacchus & Barleycorn, Ltd.
6633 Neiman Road
Shawnee, KS 66203
(913) 962-2501

Beer and Wine Hobby
180 New Boston Street
Woburn, MA 01801
(617) 933-8818

Best Brew
5236 Beach Blvd.
Jacksonville, FL 32207
(904) 396-7666

The Beverage People
840 Piner Road, #14
Santa Rosa, CA 95403
(707) 544-2520
(800) 544-1867

Brew and Wine Hobby
68 Woodbridge Avenue
East Hartford, CT 06108
(203) 528-0592

Brewhaus
4955 Ball Camp Pike
Knoxville, TN 37921
(615) 523-4615

Brew Masters, Ltd.
12266 Wilkins Avenue
Rockville, MD 20852
(301) 984-9557

Brewmeisters Supply Company
3522 W. Calavar Road
Phoenix, AZ 85023
(602) 843-4337

Cellar Wine Shop
14411 Greenwood Avenue N
Seattle, WA 98133
(206) 365-7660

Crosby and Baker
999 Main Road
Westport, MA 02790
(508) 636-5154

DeFalco's
5611 Morningside Drive
Houston, TX 77005
(800) 216-BREW

The Home Brewery
South Old Highway 65
Ozark, MO 65721
(800) 321-BREW

Home Sweet Homebrew
2008 Sansom Street
Philadelphia, PA 19103
(215) 569-9469
Fax (215) 569-4633

James Page Brewery
1300-Z Quincy Street NE
Minneapolis, MN 55413-1541
(800) 347-4042

E. C. Kraus
9001 East 24 Highway
Independence, MO 64054
(816) 254-7448

Liberty Malt Supply Company
1419 1st Avenue
Seattle, WA 98101
(206) 622-1880
(800) 990-6258
Next door to Pike Place Brewing

The Malt Shop
N. 3211 Highway S
Cascade, WI 53011
(800) 235-0026
Fax (414) 528-8167
Offers its own line of kits. Call for free catalog.

Mountain Brew
2793 South State Street
South Salt Lake City, UT 84115
(801) 487-BEER

North Denver Cellar
3475 West 32nd Avenue
Denver, CO 80211
(303) 433-5998

Ryecor Ltd.
7542 Belair Road
Baltimore, MD 21236
(410) 668-0984

Semplex of USA
4159 Thomas Avenue N
Minneapolis, MN 55412
(612) 522-0500

Something's Brewing
196 Battery Street
Burlington, VT 05401
(802) 660-9007

Stout Billy's
61 Market Street
Portsmouth, NH 03801
(603) 436-1792
(800) 392-4792
Our local brew store also offers its own line of homebrew kits. Call for a free catalog.

Williams Brewing Company
2594 Nicholson Street
San Leandro, CA 94577
(510) 895-2739

Winemakers
689 W. North Avenue
Elmhurst, IL 60126
(800) 226-BREW

BIBLIOGRAPHY

Beaumont, Stephen. *A Taste for Beer*. Pownal, VT: Storey Publishing, 1995.

Carlson, John, Jr., and Caroline Denker. "Featuring Cooper's Extract." *Zymurgy* 17, no. 1 (1994): 75.

Coy, David. "Brewferm, Glen Brew, and Young's Kits." *Zymurgy* 16, no. 5 (1993): 81.

Daniel, Steve. "American Light from Extracts." *Zymurgy* 17, no. 5, (1994): 92.

Denke, Kurt. "Brewferm Kriek and Telford's Porter." *Zymurgy* 15, no. 5 (1992): 69.

Eames, Alan D. *Secret Life of Beer: Legends, Lore, & Little-Known Facts*. Pownal, VT: Storey Publishing, 1995.

Eckhardt, Fred. *The Essentials of Beer Style*. Portland, Oregon: Fred Eckhardt Associates, 1989.

Erdoes, Richard. *1000 Remarkable Facts About Booze*. New York: Rutledge Press, 1981.

Farrel, Norman. "The Enchanting World of Malt Extract — Make the Most of It." *Zymurgy* 17, no. 5 (1994): 34.

Frane, Jeff. "How Sweet It Is — Brewing with Sugar." *Zymurgy,* Vol. 17, no. 1 (1994), p. 38.

Jackson, Michael. *Michael Jackson's Beer Companion*. Philadelphia, PA: Running Press, 1993.

———. *The New World Guide to Beer*. Philadelphia, PA: Running Press, 1988.

Ladahl, Martin. "Malt Extracts: Cause for Concern." *Brewing Techniques* 1, no. 2 (1993): 26.

La Pensee, Clive. *The Historical Companion to House-Brewing*. Beverly, UK: Montag Publications, 1990.

Leistad, Roger. *Yeast Culturing for the Homebrewer*. Ann Arbor, MI: G.W. Kent, 1983.

Lutzen, Karl F., and Mark Stevens. *Homebrew Favorites: A Coast-to-Coast Collection of More Than 240 Beer and Ale Recipes*. Pownal, VT: Storey Publishing, 1994.

Mares, William. *Making Beer.* New York: Knopf, 1984, 1994.

Miller, Dave. *Brewing the World's Great Beers.* Pownal, VT: Storey Publishing, 1992.

———— *The Complete Handbook of Home Brewing.* Pownal, VT: Storey Publishing, 1988.

———— *Dave Miller's Homebrewing Guide: Everything You Need to Know to Make Great-Tasting Beer.* Pownal, VT: Storey Publishing, 1995.

Mosher, Randy. *The Brewer's Companion.* Seattle, WA: Alephenalia Publications, 1994.

O'Neil, Carol. "Extract Magic: From Field to Kettle." *Zymurgy* 17, no. 5 (1994): 46.

Papazian, Charlie. *The Home Brewer's Companion.* New York: Avon Books, 1994.

————. *The New Complete Joy of Home Brewing.* New York: Avon Books, 1984, 1991.

Reese, M. R. *Better Beer & How to Brew It.* Pownal, VT: Storey Publishing, 1978.

Singleton, Jill. "AHA Definitive Guide: The Lowdown on Malt Extracts." *Zymurgy* 9, no. 4, (1986): 20.

Smith, Gregg. *The Beer Enthusiast's Guide.* Pownal, VT: Storey Publishing, 1994.

————. "Premier Wheat and Pale Ale Kits." *Zymurgy* 17, no. 3 (1994): 83.

Weisberg, David. *50 Great Homebrewing Tips.* Peterborough, NH: Lampman Brewing Publications, 1994.

Weix, Patrick. "Become Saccharomyces Savvy." *Zymurgy* 17, no. 2 (1994): 44.

Wood, Heather. *The Beer Directory: An International Guide.* Pownal, VT: Storey Publishing, 1995.

INDEX